# INVITATION TO THE BIBLE

*Also by Stephen Barton:*

*The Spirituality of the Gospels* (SPCK, 1992)
*People of the Passion* (Triangle/SPCK, 1994)

# INVITATION

# TO THE BIBLE

*Stephen Barton*

First published in Great Britain 1997
SPCK
Holy Trinity Church
Marylebone Road
London NW1 4DU

This book is based on material from the Aston Training Scheme module *Journeying with the Bible* and is reproduced with the permission of the Central Board of Finance of the Church of England and the Advisory Board of Ministry of the General Synod of the Church of England.

Unless otherwise indicated, all biblical quotations are taken from *The Revised Standard Version of the Bible* © 1971 and 1952.
Other biblical quotations are taken from *The New Revised Standard Version of the Bible* © 1989; and *The New English Bible* © 1961, 1970 Oxford and Cambridge University Presses.

*British Library Cataloguing in Publication Data*
A catalogue record for this book is available from the British Library

ISBN 0-281-05075-9

Typeset by Action Typesetting Ltd
Printed in Great Britain by
The Cromwell Press, Melksham, Wiltshire

To two churches who have been a source of Christian nurture
to me and many others,
and who both celebrated their centenaries in 1996

Lindfield Uniting Church
Tryon Road
Sydney
Australia

and

St John's Church
Neville's Cross
Durham
England

# Contents

# Preface

This book began life as the Bible Module for the revised syllabus of the Aston Training Scheme of the Church of England. What was asked for was something not currently available: an introduction that concerned itself less with a survey of the contents of the Bible, and more with an account of what the Bible is for and how to read it in ways that are life-giving and lead to God.

This shift in orientation was marked by a change of title. Whereas the previous module was called 'Journeying *through* the Bible', the new module was called 'Journeying *with* the Bible', since the focus now was on understanding the ways in which the Bible functions as the Scriptures of the Church for the service of God. For the present published version, the text has been revised and expanded and the title changed again: 'invitation' seems the right word for a short book which attempts to prepare the way for wise and fruitful readings of that much more profound book: the Bible itself.

I am indebted to the Reverend Roger Spiller, Principal of the Aston Training Scheme, for inviting me in 1993 to undertake the original project, and to Ms Nicola Slee, the Director of Studies at Aston, for many helpful suggestions for improvement along the way. I am grateful to them also for giving permission for the wider dissemination of this work in published form. Along with them and their colleagues, I much regret the decision of the House of Bishops to close the Scheme – not only because the new syllabus had just been put in place, but also because of the Scheme's unique and much respected contribution to pre-theological and adult education in the life of the Church over the past twenty years.[1]

Many others have contributed to this book in a variety of ways. Special thanks are due to a number of my colleagues here in Durham. Walter Moberly and Michael Gilbertson read and commented on a draft of the whole book; Ann Loades

# PREFACE

encouraged me to take the work further; and my two colleagues in New Testament, Jimmy Dunn and Loren Stuckenbruck, have been a source of ongoing expert advice and support. For valuable conversations and help at specific points, I would also like to thank Colin Crowder, Sheridan Gilley, Natalie Knödel, Peter Selby and Alan Suggate. For accepting the manuscript for publication and overseeing the process, I am very grateful to Rachel Boulding of SPCK. For friendships that sustain my labour, I think with gratitude of Sue Martin, Nicholas Watkinson, Richard and Clare Firth, Joan and Keith Twomey, George Hepburn and Jan MacGregor, Trevor and Caroline Dennis, and Michael Rusk. But, above all, it is my wife Fiona who helps make it all possible and to whom my debt is greatest.

Parts of the work were read at meetings of the Durham Centre for Theological Research and the Durham New Testament Postgraduate Seminar, at both of which I received useful comments and criticism. Other parts were presented to members of the Central Newcastle Deanery Chapter at a retreat in October 1996. An earlier version of Chapter 6 appeared as 'The Believer, the Historian and the Fourth Gospel' in *Theology*, vol. XCVI (1993), pp. 289–302. Chapter 8 was written first for a colloquium organized by Jeff Astley on 'Music, Theology and Christian Learning', held at Ushaw College in September 1994. Chapter 9 is a version of a paper presented at the Society for the Study of Christian Ethics in September 1996, and is used here with the kind permission of the editor of *Studies in Christian Ethics*.

Finally, in a book that attempts to situate the Bible and its interpretation in the life and worship of the Church, it is appropriate to express my deep appreciation to two church communities which have meant so much to me over the years, and which both, coincidentally, celebrated their centenaries in 1996: Lindfield Uniting Church in Sydney and St John's Neville's Cross in Durham. It is a great pleasure to dedicate this book to them: *ad multos annos*!

*Stephen Barton*
Durham

# 1

# Hate-mail Or Love-letter?

## or
## What kind of book is the
## Bible, and what is it for?

### *Introduction*

The Bible is a book that often generates strong emotions. This
came home to me recently as a result of a conversation with a
friend. He had been listening to a BBC radio production in
which trained actors were used to read the Bible right through
from beginning to end. As my friend listened to the reading day
after day, he was horrified by the stories of violence and genocide that occur in parts of the Old Testament. How can you call
such a book 'the Holy Bible'? he asked me. Of course, I could
see his point. I also had to admit that the violence was not
limited to parts of the Old Testament, either; for there are also
texts in the New Testament that are likely to shock the modern
reader – such as Jesus' saying to the crowds, in Luke 14.26: 'If
any one comes to me and does not hate his own father and
mother and wife and children and brothers and sisters, yes, and
even his own life, he cannot be my disciple.'

As a result, some people respond to the Bible as if it is a type
of *hate-mail*. Instead of considering the possibility that such
'hard' texts might be an invitation to look more closely for a
deeper meaning able to be located in a wider context of religious faith and practice, they can see them only as the hate-mail
of a malicious and vengeful God. A striking illustration of this

appeared in the editorial of the *Independent* of 30 November, 1994. It went as follows:

### Dramatic gesture, but not a good argument

Sir Ian McKellen, the actor and defender of homosexual rights, has caused a stir by tearing a page from a Bible in his one-man show at the Royal Lyceum Theatre in Edinburgh. It came from the book of Leviticus, and includes the sentence: 'Thou shalt not lie with mankind as with womankind: it is an abomination' (18:22). This has often been cited by conservative Christians to justify their condemnation of homosexual relationships, especially those within the Church of England. Sir Ian revealed that he removes the same page from hotel Bibles on his travels, conjuring up an image of the great actor, no sooner unpacked than getting to work with a razor. He urged his audience to do the same.

Sir Ian's hostility to the offending verse is understandable, given the ammunition it has afforded homophobic Christians. Yet his behaviour is out of character. In contrast to the militant activist Peter Tatchell, he has always been the soul of moderation in his advocacy of homosexual rights, and emerged from the debate over the age of consent with a reputation for skilful lobbying. Mutilating books does not seem to fit that image. Burning would be the logical next stage. Hitler was the specialist in that.

Perhaps the most striking aspect of the episode has been the reaction to it of a Church of England spokesman, who said: 'Generally speaking, we don't encourage people to tear pages from the Bible. It's deserving of rather more respect. But people's views are also deserving of respect.' Behind this equivocation lies, it may be surmised, a deep uncertainty with the Church of England about the historical and spiritual value of the Old Testament as a whole.

Homosexuals are not alone in being outlawed by

Leviticus: so are sexual relations with both a woman and her daughter, with a wife's sister, a neighbour's wife and just about any form of relative. Death is recommended for all transgressors. The same intolerance is on view a chapter later, in which those listed as unsuited for the priesthood are anyone blind, lame, disfigured or deformed, hunchbacked or dwarfed, or anyone with festering and running sores or damaged testicles.

In short, if all those insulted by the Old Testament were to follow Sir Ian's example, hotel Bibles would look as if they had been through a shredder. Homosexuals are not alone in bearing Leviticus a legitimate grudge. Silence is probably the best policy, but argument is preferable to vandalism, however selective it may be.

(Quoted, with gratitude, by permission of the publishers of the *Independent* newspaper.)

Whether or not we agree with the editorial's recommendation that silence is the best policy, what is quite clear is that here is an instance where, so strong are the emotions of hostility generated by the Bible, that even so distinguished an interpreter and performer of texts as Sir Ian McKellen, can respond to it only by treating it as a kind of hate-mail to be torn up and thrown away. Why is it, then, that for other people – Jews and Christians, in particular – the Bible is much more like a *love-letter*? How can it be that, apparently in spite of the difficulties in the text, Jews are so attached to the Hebrew Bible, and Christians are so attached to the Christian Bible, that both faith communities can be called 'people of the book'?

## *The Bible: the book of the Church*

Reflection on these questions makes sensible the view that it is not possible to understand the Bible properly unless we see it in relation to a much larger context. That context is the life and worship of the people of God.[1] For Jews, that means the Synagogue. For Christians, it means the Church. The Church is

3

the people, the place and the inheritance where Christians learn what the Bible is really about and how to read it wisely. To put it another way, the Bible is the book of the Church. The Bible helps to make the Church what it is and, at the same time, it is the Church that acknowledges the Bible as Scripture and provides the wisdom and skills that allow it to speak as God's love-letter to the world. But to take this further, we need to take one step back. We need, that is, to *start with God.*

In the faith of Christians, God is love and the source of all life; and this love and life of God is abundant and overflowing. It overflows within the triune being of God. It overflows also in creation, election, redemption, and new creation. To put it another way, God has not kept his love to himself; he has not kept it a secret. Rather, God has revealed his love and his life – in creation, in Israel, in Christ, in the Church, and in the world. Christians call the Bible 'Scripture' or 'Holy Writ' because it bears unique testimony to this triune God who is love.

When we come together as the people of God to worship God, we celebrate God's love and share in the life God gives. To assist us in that celebration, we use what one liturgical theologian has called three 'holy things': water, bread and wine, and words.[2] Each of these is a source of life, because each of these *brings us into contact* with God-in-Christ-through-the-Spirit. In the water of baptism our sins are cleansed and we are united with Christ in his death and resurrection. In the eating of the bread and drinking of the wine we are nourished by our participation in the life-giving body and blood of Christ. And then there are words – in our invocations, hymns, prayers, readings, preaching and blessings. Like the water for washing and the bread and wine for eating and drinking, the words also are given by God for our nourishment. They are part of God's divine hospitality which nurtures and enlivens us and makes communion with God possible.

This is how we ought to understand the Bible and what it is for. Just as baptism brings us into contact with Christ as we die and rise with him, and just as the Eucharist brings us into contact with Christ as we eat his flesh and drink his blood, so too the Bible brings us into contact with Christ as we read its testimony to the one God, Father, Son and Holy Spirit. For the Bible is made up of words that bear witness to the Living Word, Jesus Christ. That is why the Bible is so important. Not only as history, nor as great literature – though it may be both of these – but as words that testify concerning the Living Word who gives us life. To put it in terms of the powerful image used by Martin Luther, the Bible is like the manger and the swaddling clothes which contained within them God's precious gift to the world, Jesus the Christ.

## Reading wisely

The question that follows must be: how, then, may we read the Bible in ways that bring life rather than death, or that allow it to speak like a love-letter rather than hate-mail? There is no short answer to this, because the Bible is a very unusual book, itself a collection of unusual books written over a long period of time. However, three points are important as rough 'ground rules'.[3]

First, and of greatest importance, to read the Bible wisely we need to be set on loving the triune God with all our heart, soul, mind and strength, and on loving our neighbours as ourselves (cf. Deuteronomy 6.5; Leviticus 19.18; Luke 10.27). The ultimate purpose of the Bible itself is to summon us to this twofold love: so it makes good sense to say that we will best hear this summons if our hearts are inclined already in that direction. This is another way of saying that the way we respond to what the Bible says is partly a matter of personal character, disposition and intention. If our hearts are open to receive God's love and to be transformed into God's image, then, like Christians down the centuries, we will find that God's Spirit speaks to us through the words of Scripture, bringing us into life-giving contact with God's living and life-giving Word. It is the reader who is already being transformed into the likeness of Christ who is able to discern most truly the testimony of Scripture to Christ and the Christian way. The apostle Paul put it this way, in 1 Corinthians 2.14–16 (NRSV):

Now we have received not the spirit of the world, but the Spirit that is from God, so that we might understand the gifts bestowed on us by God. And we speak of these things in words not taught by human wisdom but taught by the Spirit, interpreting spiritual truths to those who are spiritual. Those who are unspiritual do not receive the gifts of the Spirit, for they are foolishness to them, and they are unable to understand them because they are spiritually discerned. Those who are spiritual discern all things, and they are themselves subject to no one else's scrutiny. 'For who has known the mind of the Lord so as to instruct him?' But we have the mind of Christ.

To put it another way, because the Bible was written 'from faith for faith', the only way it can be understood and appreciated fully is if it is read 'from faith for faith', under the guidance of the Holy Spirit. In fact, the Bible is often read in other ways – as a book of rules, or an historical record, or ancient literature, or a classic of western civilization. Now it may be all of these things. Yet none of these categories does full justice to the kind of book the Bible is and what the Bible is for in the faith of Christians. To use an image from wood-working, if we want to understand the Bible properly, we need to read with the grain rather than against it. 'Going with the grain' means reading the Bible with a view to growth in love for God and neighbour, since that is what the Bible is for.

A second and related 'ground rule' is that we cannot really read the Bible wisely on our own. We need the help that is found in friendships, communities and institutions of one kind or another. Such relationships, communities and institutions contribute a number of things. They embody for us in quite practical ways and by personal example, past and present, what it means to read the Bible wisely. They preserve memories and traditions about how the Bible has been interpreted in the past. They impart the linguistic skills and historical knowledge that inform our understanding of the biblical text and its historical context. They help shape us in the qualities of character that make reading with discernment possible.

Because the Bible is the book of the Church, it is the community of the Church in particular that should provide the primary context for reading the Bible appropriately and coming to a mature understanding of the truth to which it testifies. It is, above all, within the life of the Church that we can learn the skills, virtues and wisdom that make it possible to read the Bible well.[4]

Of course, the relationship between Bible and Church is not by any means a simple one. At some points in Christian history it has been felt that the Church has hindered a true hearing of what the Bible says. The sixteenth-century Reformation was one such point, with Luther's slogan, *sola scriptura* ('scripture alone'), representing an important corrective to what he saw as the unreformed magisterium of the Church. At other points in history, it has been felt that people have lost their way in the Christian life because they have tried to interpret the Bible independently of the wisdom and authority of the Church. This is the concern that comes to the surface, for example, in present-day anxieties about doing 'biblical studies' in the free-thinking ethos of a secular university.[5] But none of this undercuts the more straightforward point being made here: that learning to read the Bible wisely is something that takes place best within the ongoing life, worship and practical wisdom of the Church – so long, of course, as the Church remains guided and inspired by the Holy Spirit.

A third relevant 'ground rule' is the need for practice. In some ways, learning to read the Bible is like learning to read music or play a musical instrument. These are skills that require time and constant practice. To make progress in musicianship, we also need a trained teacher to guide us and pass on the skills and wisdom that he or she has learned, in turn, from someone else. It is also the case that the more difficult the instrument, the more practice is required and the more important it is to learn as much as possible from how other people do it, especially other people who do it well.

It is a similar situation with the Bible. The Bible is a complicated book, written over a very long period of time in three ancient languages by many different and mostly unknown authors using a wide variety of literary genres. Therefore it is not surprising that it is difficult to read the Bible with an adequate appreciation of what it is trying to say. Its meanings are multiple, and its significance alters with changing historical and cultural circumstances. So, to read it well requires constant practice under the guidance of people with the appropriate gifts – theologians, preachers, teachers and any other people of spiritual maturity who show by the quality of their discipleship of Christ that their reading of Scripture has brought them into contact with the life-giving Word. Thus the point we are making here is that learning to read the Bible wisely is part of our Christian discipleship within the fellowship of the Church. As such, it is a full-time business.

We have already used the image of learning to play music to give some idea of what this process is like. A different image, though, is used by Christian ethicist Stanley Hauerwas. It is the image of learning how to be a bricklayer. What Hauerwas says is very pertinent to our point about the need for practice in learning to read the Bible wisely:

> To learn to lay brick, it is not sufficient for you to be told how to do it, but you must learn a multitude of skills that are coordinated into the activity of laying brick. ... Moreover, it is not enough to be told how to hold a trowel, how to spread mortar, or how to frog the mortar, but in order to lay brick you must hour after hour, day by day, lay brick.
>
> Of course, learning to lay brick involves not only learning myriad skills, but also a language that forms and is formed by those skills. ... You cannot learn to lay brick without learning to talk 'right'.
>
> The language embodies the history of the craft of bricklaying. So when you learn to be a bricklayer you are not learning a craft de novo but rather being initiated into a history. For example, bricks have different names ... to denote different qualities that make a difference about

how one lays them. These differences are discovered often by apprentices being confronted with new challenges, making mistakes, and then being taught how to do it by the more experienced.

All of this indicates that to lay brick you must be initiated into the craft of bricklaying by a master craftsman.

(Stanley Hauerwas, *After Christendom?* (Nashville: Abingdon Press, 1991), pp 101–2.)

If learning to 'lay brick' is not quite as straightforward as it looks and requires being apprenticed to a master craftsman, it is likely that learning to read and understand a book like the Bible is not so straightforward either! Sometimes people give the impression that it is a very simple matter: that the Bible is a 'plain book' which anyone can read. At the most basic level, this may well be the case. Certainly, parts of the Bible contain what look like simple, easy-to-understand stories which speak directly to anyone who reads or hears them. Think of Adam and Eve, Noah's Ark, David and Goliath, the nativity stories, the parables of Jesus, Paul's missionary journeys, and the like. Certainly also, there is an important underlying theological concern at stake about salvation and the nature of the Church. This is the fundamental point that the love of God is not restricted to privileged groups of one kind or another – not even people who can read the Bible in Hebrew and Greek – but that it is open to people from every background and walk of life.

Having said this, however, it is also true to say that the Bible is the kind of book that is not exhausted by one easy read-through. On the contrary, it is the kind of book that invites constant return to be read and re-read in order that the story it tells can be understood more fully, and that the mystery of God to which it testifies can be encountered at ever deeper levels. This is a process that requires wisdom, skill, guidance and practice – as well as divine inspiration – if it is to be done well.

## Conclusion

An important text for understanding what the Bible is for and how to read it wisely is the well-known passage from 2 Timothy 3.14–17 (NEB):

> But for your part, stand by the truths you have learned and are assured of. Remember from whom you learned them; remember that from early childhood you have been familiar with the sacred writings which have power to make you wise and lead you to salvation through faith in Jesus Christ. Every inspired scripture has its use for teaching the truth and refuting error, or for reformation of manners and discipline in right living, so that the man who belongs to God may be efficient and equipped for good work of every kind.

Over the past one hundred years, this text has been 'hijacked' in some Christian circles by being made to serve a doctrine of biblical infallibility.[6] For some Protestants at the end of the nineteenth century (and subsequently), the newly promulgated Roman Catholic dogma of papal infallibility had to be counteracted, and the most effective way of doing so was to insist on an alternative source of authority, that of Scripture. Hence the doctrine of the infallibility of the Bible. But this kind of argument about whether or not the Bible really is infallible, and if so in what sense, usually ends up becoming a serious distraction from a mature understanding of the place of the Bible in the life of faith, an understanding that is truly *catholic*, and can therefore be shared by Protestants and Roman Catholics and Orthodox alike.

Read in a broader theological context, the text from 2 Timothy helps us to see again that the main purpose of the Bible as Christian Scripture is to lead us to faith in Christ and to guide us in the life of faith. It also reinforces the point made earlier that the truths to which the Scriptures bear witness are best learned in the community of faith, from people who have tested them out and who know from experience what will 'make you wise and lead you to salvation'. Significant in this connection is the acknowledgement given at the opening of 2 Timothy to the role of Timothy's grandmother Lois and his mother Eunice in providing him with Christian nurture, instruction and example (2 Timothy 1.5). Timothy has not had to go it alone; he has learned the craft of Christian discipleship and wise reading of Scripture within the communal context of his own extended household.

This conception of what Scripture is for and how its truth is learned has the important corollary that private interpretations (or the interpretations of one particular group) always need to be tested out by asking questions like: Does this reading lead to faith in Christ and good works towards my neighbours, or does it undermine them? Does this interpretation fit with what the Church down the ages has come to confess as true, or is it a departure from that confession? Does this understanding build up the Church and strengthen its witness, or does it weaken the Church?

Of course, this understanding of the Bible and how to read it wisely is a quite general one, but it is none the worse for that. On the contrary, a broad, general understanding allows us to see more specific problems and issues in a proper Christian perspective. On the one hand, such an understanding helps us to recognize what is most important, instead of being distracted by 'battles for the Bible' that may not be worth fighting. On the other hand, it helps us to avoid interpretations that turn the Bible from being the love-letter from God it is meant to be into a text to which people can respond only as hate-mail.

# 2

# The Art Of Interpretation

or

## When is a text biblical
## without being Christian?

## *Introduction*

The case of Sir Ian McKellen referred to at the beginning of
Chapter 1 shows that the Bible is in some ways a 'difficult' book,
full of 'problem texts' that can very easily be misunderstood,
even by people who are intelligent and sophisticated. To make
true understanding possible, interpretation of the text is essential. That is to say, bridges have to be built between the ancient
texts (in their original languages of Hebrew, Aramaic and
Greek) and people trying to make sense of these texts today.
Even when the literal sense of the text has been established with
some degree of certainty, the question of the meaning or significance of the text *as 'word of God' for us today* has still to be
addressed. It is time, therefore, to outline some important principles of scriptural interpretation which have been shaped and
developed by theologians from the very beginnings of the
Church, often in conjunction with the work of the rabbis and
their forebears on the interpretation of the Hebrew Bible.

## *Reading in the context of our life in and for God*

One important principle of scriptural interpretation is that
Scripture must be interpreted *theologically and theocentrically*. This
means that judgements about the meaning and truth of what the
Bible says have to be evaluated in accordance with our prior,
Christian understanding of God and the nature of reality. What
the Bible 'says' and how the Bible 'speaks' to us today are not

necessarily one and the same. To put it another way, a text may be biblical in the sense of 'coming from somewhere in the Bible' without necessarily being 'Christian' in the sense of 'according with what the Church down the ages has come to believe to be true'.[1]

Sir Ian McKellen's mistake, perhaps, was to assume that because a text comes from the Bible, Christians believe it to be 'gospel' – when in fact *it is the gospel that helps Christians to evaluate what the Bible says!* In other words, for the Bible to speak to us today, what it says needs to be interpreted theologically. It is our understanding and experience of God and the nature of reality – mediated to us partly through the testimony of Scripture itself – that provides us with the framework and the criteria for encountering the living and life-giving Word of God through the words of the text.

This theological and theocentric approach has a number of advantages. First and foremost, it is in line with the true content of Scripture itself. As the literary critic Gabriel Jasopovici put it recently, the Bible is 'the Book of God'. In other words, reading theocentrically helps to prevent us from getting sidetracked on to issues of history or literature or science – issues that may only be peripheral to the Bible's main subject: the revelation of God. After all, the first words of Genesis are, 'In the beginning God created the heavens and the earth'; the first words of Mark's Gospel are, 'The beginning of the gospel of Jesus Christ the Son of God'; the first words of the Gospel of John are, 'In the beginning was the Word and the Word was with God and the Word was God'; and the Epistle to the Hebrews opens with the programmatic testimony, 'In many and various ways God spoke of old to our fathers by the prophets; but in these last days he has spoken to us by a Son'. If, as these texts suggest, the Bible consists of written testimony to divine revelation, then it makes most sense to go to it with just that in view, open to the possibility of hearing God speak.

Another advantage of the theocentric approach is that it is truest to the primary context in and for which Scripture is read, namely the worship of God by God's people, who are the Body of Christ. This point is made also by Dan Hardy and David Ford, in their book, *Jubilate*:

> The contents of the Bible are very varied. It can be read for its history, its language and literature, its world-views, its ethics, its religion, its sociology, its wisdom, its prophecy, and much else. Some ways of approaching it catch more of its substance than others, though none can claim to be comprehensive. Our own key to interpreting it ... is as a book primarily related to God and written by people who were engaged in praising him. It was produced in a context of active commitment to God over many centuries, so the dynamics of this relationship are vital to understanding it.
> (Dan Hardy and David Ford, *Jubilate. Theology in Praise* (London, Darton, Longman and Todd, 1984), p. 24.)

What this statement suggests also is that reading the Bible as Scripture within the worshipping community is an ongoing process in the context of communion with God. Therefore Scripture is not static, and interpretation is not a matter of reciting old formulas as if they are set in stone. Rather, reading and interpreting Scripture is a dynamic process. It is an integral part of discerning the truth about God and how to live for God that requires inspiration, imagination, wisdom and practical engagement.

The theocentric approach also keeps scriptural interpretation in the public domain. This is so because theological interpretation involves adopting a framework capable of articulation and defence according to the acknowledged rational and critical standards of the day. This is an important safeguard against various kinds of Christian obscurantism or antiquarianism, where the claims of Scripture remain meaningful only for members of an isolated religious circle; and the well-meant concern to protect Scripture and doctrine from a godless world has the disastrous effect of creating an unbridgeable gap with very little possibility of contact between the two sides. The results of this gap are very damaging. On the one side, Christian interpretation can lose touch with reality and reason and become vulnerable to irrationality or fanaticism. On the other, the testimony of Scripture to God's Living Word is unnecessarily obscured in the eyes of those in the world around us who do not have Christian faith, but who may be on the look-out for (what Peter Berger called) signals of transcendence.

If we read Scripture theocentrically, we are liable to discover that what Scripture does is to identify God for us in ways that take us quite by surprise, transform the way we see things, and make us different kinds of people. In other words, we discover divine grace and providence. Just think how surprising so many of the stories are from both Old and New Testaments. For example, God creates the heavens and the earth, but the pinnacle of his activity is his resting on the seventh day. He determines to destroy the earth on account of human iniquity, but rescues from the deluge a single household in an ark. He calls Abraham to be the 'father of many nations', but commands him to sacrifice his only son Isaac. He is Lord of the nations, but chooses the insignificant Israelites to be his chosen people. He delivers the Israelites from the power of the Egyptians only to make them wander in the wilderness for forty years. God's freedom and lordship are unrivalled, but he exercises that lordship by becoming incarnate in the Galilean teacher, Jesus of Nazareth. He is the source of all wisdom, but conveys that wisdom in a mystery: the crucifixion of his own Son. He empowers the Church to preach and heal, yet the power they experience comes in simple gatherings for prayer, Scripture reading and table-fellowship, and in apostolic experiences of hardship and suffering. The point is: we are likely to miss the surprise and the 'dynamite' in the text if we come to it in the wrong spirit asking the wrong questions.

It is important to add that theocentric *means* theocentric. The problem with some Christian readings is that they are too narrowly focused on Jesus – as if 'Jesus says' tells us all we need to know. In Christian faith, however, the truth about Jesus is wider and deeper than what Jesus himself said and did (cf. John

15

16.12–15; 21.25). This is not necessarily to say that the truth about Jesus contradicts what he himself said and did. Rather, the truth about Jesus is revealed more fully *in relation to the mystery we call God.* The consequence of this is that a properly Christian reading is one that is first and foremost theocentric and trinitarian. This is the only way to avoid readings of Scripture like those of the early heretic Marcion (and of some Christians today) that have no room for the Old Testament, or that treat Old Testament law as negative, restrictive and altogether superseded by Christ, or that see Old Testament prophecy as without value in itself except as predicting events which, once fulfilled, render it redundant.

The consequences for faith of such an approach to the Bible are serious and we need to be aware of the possibilities. One tendency is for faith in the triune God to become reduced to 'personal relationship with Jesus' in such a way that the mystery of faith is sentimentalized. Another tendency is for faith and individual salvation to float adrift from their proper moorings in the doctrine of the righteousness of the God who calls into being a people to do his will. A related tendency is for a wedge to be driven between Christian freedom and the practice of holiness. At the same time, it is easy for the Christian tradition to lose a sense of its roots in and kinship with Judaism, with anti-semitism never far away as a result. For all these reasons, a lot is at stake.

Finally, a theocentric reading, more than any other approach, makes it possible to read the Bible as one book, taking both Testaments seriously and together. North American Presbyterian theologian Daniel Migliore has put it this way:

> *Christians read Scripture as witness to the activity of the triune God.* The God of the biblical witness is God the Father who has created the heavens and the earth, God the Son who has become the mediator for the whole world, God the Holy Spirit who brings new life and freedom. In response to the activity of the triune God, men and women are called to repentance and faith. They are

summoned and empowered to become partners in God's
liberating and reconciling activity in the world.
(Daniel Migliore, *Faith Seeking Understanding* (Grand
Rapids, Eerdmans, 1991), p. 53; the italic is his.)

One of the striking things about Migliore's statement about
how Christians read the Bible is its credal quality: 'God the
Father ... God the Son ... God the Holy Spirit ...'. This is not
coincidental. It is another way of making the point that we made
earlier when we said that it is the gospel that helps Christians
interpret and evaluate what the Bible says. For the creed – or,
more broadly, what the Church Fathers called the 'rule of faith'
(*regula fidei*) – is a summary of the gospel; thus it provides the
framework that enables us to read Scripture as true testimony to
the triune God.[2]

## *The literal and the spiritual*

A second principle of scriptural interpretation is that, because
the Bible is a book from the past and (at least to some extent)
about the past, it is important to make use of historical methods
of reading. These methods give us access to the literal meaning
of the Bible – i.e. to the original meaning intended by the
authors of those individual texts that make up the text as a
whole. In addition, because the Bible is not just an historical
*source*, but also a significant *text* – much of which takes the form
of realistic narrative – it is important to make use of literary ways
of reading in order to understand it. Whereas historical method
helps us to understand the Bible in relation to the original
contexts in and for which it was written, literary method helps us
to appreciate how the Bible communicates as text. To put it
another way, historical method opens up the world 'behind' the
text, while literary method opens up the world 'within' the text
– how the text 'works' as narrative, poetry, parable, law, epistle,
apocalypse, and so on.[3]
Historical study is important theologically. For one thing, it
highlights the particularity of divine revelation, in the life of the

nation of Israel, in the life, death and resurrection of Jesus of Nazareth, and in the life of the apostolic Church. It also highlights the fact that the biblical narrative is not just realistic fiction – even if it has fictional elements – but refers at many points to realities behind or outside the text, realities that are important for the truthfulness of Christian faith and that historical research can help to validate.

Another reason for its importance is that historical criticism makes us aware that the biblical writers were thoroughly conditioned by their place and time in the past. There is a distance that separates them from us: a distance of chronology, language, thought-forms, culture, social patterns and world-view. Historical interpretation mediates between the past and the present. It helps us to understand the texts in their own historical contexts and to avoid the misunderstandings and confusions that come from anachronistic readings where the sense of distance is lost.

This sense of distance and of the 'strangeness' of the Bible has the potential for acting as a corrective both to simplistically supernaturalist doctrines of biblical inspiration and to equally simplistic anti-supernaturalist rejection of what the Bible is all about. The irony of Sir Ian McKellen's critical reaction to the Book of Leviticus is that his reading of Leviticus is not critical enough! For if he had read the text with the sensitivity that historical criticism is designed to make possible, he might have been able to understand what it was in the conditions and world-view of the time that made possible the particular view of purity and the particular construction of gender relations contained in the text. He might also have been able to recognize that major changes in the human condition and world-view since antiquity require that notions of purity and ways of constructing gender relations be understood in ways significantly different today.[4]

But if historical and literary criticism are important for the task of interpreting Scripture, equally important in a Christian context is the recognition that historical and literary criticism need to be used *not as ends in themselves*, but in order to enable a better hearing and a more faithful appropriation of God's

Word today. In this way, the various forms of criticism used in the academic study of the Bible can be seen not as some kind of threat, but as a gift to aid us in discerning not only the literal (i.e. historical) sense, but also the spiritual sense to which it points.

The testimony of Bishop John V. Taylor corroborates this whole point quite powerfully:

> It was [while] reading English and history at Cambridge that ... I began to appreciate the relation between the meaning of any piece of literature and the historical situation within which it was written. I learned to guess at the period, and even the author of an unidentified passage of prose or poetry from its style. I could tell myth from epic, romance from scholarly chronicle, a spontaneous report from a well-worn anecdote, and both from a literary narrative. Instinctively I could recognize all these, and many other kinds of writing, in the Old and New Testaments; and I wanted to read them as such, as myth or epic or song or history or sermon, if that was their nature. For I felt that was how God had intended them to be the vehicle of his voice.
>
> As I went on to take a degree in theology I discovered the prophets of Israel. Up till then they had merely contributed some purple passages to my anthology of personal comfort, reproof and doctrine. Now I was exhilarated by the distinct individualities that emerged from their recorded outbursts, their heroic outbursts against social wrongs, political follies, religious apostasy, their daring vision of a suffering, passionate God. I felt like someone well stocked with Shakespearean tags, who had just emerged, for the first time in his life, from a performance of one of Shakespeare's plays.
>
> (John V. Taylor, 'Divine Revelation through Human Experience', in John V. Taylor *et al.*, *Bishops on the Bible* (London, Triangle/SPCK, 1993), pp. 2–3.)

19

We will have occasion in a subsequent chapter to take up the idea of 'performance' again. What is important to note here is Bishop Taylor's testimony to the enormous spiritual gain he experienced in learning to interpret the Bible through the lenses of history and literature.

The same point can be made in another way. If we take as an analogy the debates in the early Church about the true nature of Christ as both fully human and yet also fully divine, we can think of historical criticism as helping us to recognize similarly that the Bible has, so to speak, 'two natures'. On the one hand, it is a unique witness to God and a unique source of knowledge of God. On the other, it is treasure in earthen vessels, a text conditioned *in toto* by the historical conditions in which it was produced and which shaped the long process of its formation into a scriptural canon.

This is crucial from a theological point of view, since it follows that the 'plain meaning' of the text is by no means necessarily identifiable in a straightforward way with the *Christian theological meaning(s)* of the text. It means that the understanding of a text for what it may contribute to the knowledge and love of God is something that can be discerned only after the rigorous application of the canons of Christian judgement. The warning words of John Bowker are salutory:

> The consequences of treating Scripture as though history and personality make no difference to the words and content of Scripture have been, in Christian history, horrendous. By lifting a text from its context and treating it as a timeless truth, Christians claimed scriptural warrant for their murder of Jews (Matthew 27.25); by lifting a text, Christians found warrant for burning women whom they regarded as witches (Exodus 22.18); by lifting a text, Christians justified slavery and apartheid (Genesis 9.25); by lifting a text Christians found warrant for executing homosexuals (Leviticus 20.13); by lifting a text (Genesis 3.16), Christians found warrant for the subordination of women to men, so that they came to be

regarded as 'a sort of infant', incapable of taking charge
of their own bodies, finances and lives.
(John Bowker, *A Year to Live* (London, SPCK, 1991),
pp. 14–15.)

So 'criticism', in this context, is not a negative task of trying to
'pick holes' in Scripture in order to undermine what Scripture
has to say. Rather, it is the positive task of *wise discernment* of the
meaning and significance of Scripture for today using the best
tools available.

## Reading contextually

A third major principle is the importance of interpreting
Scripture in the context of the present. This allows the Bible to
be read not just as historical record, but also as divine revelation,
a medium for the revelation of God's will for living in the world
today – which is what is meant when we call the Bible 'Scripture'.
Reading Scripture contextually in this sense means interpreting
the text in relation to what is happening on 'this side' of the
text. This has several dimensions.

First, there is *the individual and personal context,* in which we
read the Bible in the belief that God speaks to us and meets our
needs through it. Here, Scripture has a direct, existential dimension. A classic, biblical expression of this comes in Psalm
119.97–105:

Oh, how I love thy law!
It is my meditation all the day.
Thy commandment makes me wiser than my enemies,
for it is ever with me.
I have more understanding than all my teachers,
for thy testimonies are my meditation. ...

How sweet are thy words to my taste,
sweeter than honey to my mouth!

21

Through thy precepts I get understanding;
therefore I hate every false way.
Thy word is a lamp to my feet
and a light to my path.

This text captures in a nutshell the sense of reverence for Scripture common to Jewish and Christian believers alike. It captures also the sense that frequent and ongoing meditation on the sacred text is nourishing and life-giving for each individual reader. There is even the suggestion that the text becomes part of the reader ('How sweet are thy words to my taste, sweeter than honey to my mouth!'), a metaphor that is developed further elsewhere (cf. Jeremiah 1.9; 15.16; Ezekiel 2.8—3.3). There is also the idea that God's Word, in the form of the text of Scripture, makes God present to the one who meditates on it, and accompanies him or her along life's way.

No wonder, then, that the regular reading of Scripture has become an important feature of the lifestyle of Christian people, lay and ordained. It is a principle enshrined in Thomas Cranmer's Introduction to *The Book of Common Prayer*, where he says, 'Concerning the Service of the Church':

> that the Clergy, and especially such as were Ministers in the congregation, should (by often reading and meditation in God's Word) be stirred up to godliness themselves ... and further that the people (by daily hearing of Holy Scripture read in the Church) might continually profit more and more in the knowledge of God and be more inflamed with the love of his true religion.

When we come to more modern times, we have the moving testimony of Dietrich Bonhoeffer, who also placed great stress on the importance of regular, personal meditation on the biblical text. Interestingly, his advice comes in instruction on how to read the psalm we have already referred to, Psalm 119. Bonhoeffer says:

Psalm 119 will be especially difficult for us, perhaps, because of its length and uniformity. Here a very slow, quiet, patient advance from word to word, from sentence to sentence, will help us. Then we will recognize that the apparent repetitions are ever new variations on a single theme – love for God's Word. As this love can never end, neither can the words which confess it. They are to accompany us through an entire lifetime and, in their simplicity, become the prayer of the child, the adult and the old person.

(Dietrich Bonhoeffer, *Meditating on the Word* (Cambridge, MA, Cowley, 1986), p. 10.)

This brings us to a second aspect of 'reading contextually': *the ecclesial context* of interpretation. This means reading the Bible as the Church's book, where the Bible is understood as God's gift to the Church to sustain and guide it, and where the Church and its traditions provide wisdom and experience as to what constitutes a good or true reading. Daniel Migliore puts it this way: 'Thus, to interpret Scripture contextually means to listen to its story in and with the community of faith ... confidently expecting that the Spirit of God will again speak to us through the biblical witness.'[5]

A very good sense of what this means is given by Thomas Merton, who speaks of how the 'I' of the psalmist comes to stand for the individual and the Church:

The kings of strange desert tribes have survived in the psalms; they were the enemies of Israel. Their mysterious names do not mean anything definite to us. These kings emerged from the verses of psalms like the weird symbolic enemies that menace us in dreams and fade away. They are the powers of evil that are still around us today. We know that Sisera is dead with a tent peg in his temple, and Jabin's bones long ago whitened in the ravine of Cisson. Yet Jabin and Sisera still rise up to plague us though they cannot prevail. But we know, on the nights when their names pass before us, in the small hours, at the chanting of Mattins, that the old battles we are celebrating are more than ever actual. Actual too are the same miracles by which Israel overcame her enemies and entered glorious through divided Jordan to occupy the Promised Land. These battles and these victories go on without ceasing, generation after generation and century by century, because the whole church is still passing out of Egypt, company by company. The shining tribes of Israel are still crossing the desert in the slow interminable march that Balaam saw from his mountain when his curse against them choked in his gullet and turned into a song of praise.

(Quoted by David Hope in his essay, 'Prayer and the Scriptures', in John V. Taylor, et al., Bishops on the Bible (London, Triangle/SPCK, 1993), pp. 75–6.)

What is noticeable in Merton's words is both a sense of the distance separating readers today from the world of ancient Israel lying behind the Bible, and at the same time a sense of the immediacy of the text and the realities to which the text bears witness. The gulf is both acknowledged and transcended. There is in Merton's reading of the Old Testament both historical and literary awareness and, with the aid of that awareness, contact with the text at a deeper and more profound level.

This is what the French philosopher Paul Ricoeur describes as reading from the position of a 'second naïveté'.[6] The 'first naïveté' of simplistic literalism is transformed through critical insight into something deeper: a contact with the text that is both closer and better attuned. As a result, the story of Israel is able to speak to and of the story of the Church, and the story of the Church is able to resonate with the story of Israel. The text is not followed slavishly or believed in 'literally' (i.e. at the surface level only), but neither does the text become a 'dead letter' or something to be treated at will. Rather, in the liturgical context of the reading of Scripture in divine worship ('in the small hours, at the chanting of Mattins'), the Old Testament takes on new life as a medium for revelation and instruction about the nature of the Christian way.

But as well as the individual context and the ecclesial context, there is the wider context of *human experience in the world-at-large*, in particular (as we have come to learn from Liberation Theology), the experience of the marginalized, the poor and the suffering. Biblical interpretation that takes place only at the level of the needs of the individual – or only at the level of the Church – is legitimate and necessary, but does not go far enough. It is not contextual enough. For it fails to reckon with the fact that, from a theological perspective, the Bible concerns the revelation of God's love and justice in relation to the whole created order as it groans in bondage to sin and longs for redemption and reconciliation (cf. Romans 8). The Bible belongs not just to the Church, but to the world as well. In that sense, it is a public document and has a legitimate place, not only in public institutions like colleges and universities, but also in the wider social domain, wherever truth is contested, wherever power is exercised, and wherever justice is sought.

From a Liberation Theology perspective, insight into what constitutes a wise reading of Scripture in the context of society-at-large is most likely to come from those who read Scripture from the social margins – from Jews, with their long history of suffering due to anti-semitism; from blacks, who have suffered slavery and apartheid; from women, who have suffered inequality and abuse in societies organized in line with patriarchy; and from the poor of the Third World, who suffer the social and economic injustice that arises from colonialism and the imbalance of power and wealth between North and South.[7]

However, when liberation theologians speak of 'the hermeneutical privilege of the poor', what they have in mind is not some kind of claim to moral or religious superiority on the part of the poor, but a recognition that, because the God of the Bible is a righteous God who is for the poor and the marginalized in a quite unlimited way, experiences of poverty, suffering and powerlessness provide *a special opportunity* for understanding the message of the Bible, a message that power and privilege easily obscure (cf. Philippians 3.7–11).

What this means in practice is described by the Brazilian theologian Carlos Mesters in an article on 'The Use of the Bible in Christian Communities of the Common People'. There he describes what a difference is made to reading the Bible when the Bible is allowed to interact with both the life of the common people and with the realities of the wider world that impinge so heavily upon them:

> We find three elements in the common people's interpretation of the Bible: the Bible itself, the community, and reality (i.e. the real-life situation of the people and the surrounding world). With these three elements they seek to hear what the word of God is saying. And for them the word of God is not just the Bible. The word of God is within reality and it can be discovered there with the help of the Bible. When one of the three elements is missing, however, interpretation of the Bible makes no progress and enters into crisis. The Bible loses its function. When the three elements are present and enter the process of interpretation, then you get the situation that I encountered when I gave a course in Ceará. The people asked me to tell them the stories of Abraham, Moses, Jeremiah, and Jesus. That is what I did. But in their group discussions and full meetings, the Bible disappeared. They hardly ever talked about the Bible. Instead they talked about real life and their concrete struggles. So at the nightly review the local priest asked them what they had learned that day. They quickly got to talking about real life. No one said anything about the Bible. Ye gods, I thought to myself, where did I go wrong? This is supposed to be a course on the Bible and all they talk about is real life. Should I feel upset and frustrated, or should I be satisfied? Well, I decided to take it easy and feel satisfied because the Bible had achieved its purpose.

Like salt, it had disappeared into the pot and spiced the whole meal.

(Carlos Mesters, 'The Use of the Bible in Christian Communities of the Common People', in S. Torres and J. Eagleson, eds, *The Challenge of Basic Christian Communities* (New York, Orbis, 1981), pp. 199–200.)

## Conclusion

The art of interpreting the Bible is just that: an art. It is not an exact science – if there is such a thing! But neither is it a matter just of aesthetics and critical appreciation. Still less is it a matter of 'anything goes' or 'your guess is as good as mine'. Rather, as we have seen, interpreting the Bible is an act of Christian discernment of the will of God in the context of faithful discipleship in the fellowship of the Church for the sake of the world.

Thus interpreting the Bible involves the coming together of two horizons: the horizon of the reader in his or her own context of life, and the horizon of the text in all its strangeness and otherness. For there is a proper sense – as Karl Barth pointed out – in which it must be the case theologically that it is not only we who read and interpret Scripture, but also that Scripture reads and interprets us.[8]

# 3

# Two Testaments, One Bible

## or
## Why should Christians read
## the Old Testament?

### *Introduction*

A striking feature of the Christian Bible is that not only does it contain two main divisions, or 'Testaments', each of which is further divided into individual 'books', but also that the two Testaments are very unequal in size. Thus in the edition of the Revised Standard Version known as *The Common Bible*,[1] the Old Testament and Apocrypha take up about 1100 pages, while the New Testament takes up only 250 pages! This means that, in terms of sheer size, the Old Testament is approximately four times longer than the New.

Given this massive inbalance in favour of the Old Testament in the Bible, how could the reading of the Old Testament by Christians even be an issue? In fact, as many people are coming to recognize, the reading of the Old Testament is in crisis.[2] If that is indeed so, then the unity of the Bible is at risk. If the unity of the Bible is at risk, then the coherence of Christian faith and doctrine is at risk also, since faith and doctrine have taken shape down the ages in constant dialogue with both Old and New Testaments. Therefore, if our faith journey with the Bible is to be a journey with the *whole* Bible, rather than some truncated or bowdlerized form of it, we need to spend some time considering how, if at all, the two Testaments speak as one, and what part the Old Testament plays.

It is important to add that this complex of issues has been with the Church from its earliest days.[3] The controversy was fought out on at least two fronts. On the one hand, there were the controversies generated by conservative 'Judaizing' Christians, who sought to maintain observance of Old Testament law and thereby keep the Church within Judaism. On the other hand, there was the radicalism of Marcion and the Gnostics in the second century, who sought to dispense with the Jewish heritage and the creator God of the Old Testament by rejecting the Old Testament and accepting as canonical or normative only a small number of New Testament texts. These controversies focused the problem of the canon of Scripture and its interpretation and helped the Church to recognize that the issue at stake was a matter not just of the place of the Old Testament, but, much more seriously, the identity of the Church and the nature of the Christian understanding of God.

The solution of Church Fathers like Justin Martyr and Irenaeus was to reject both conservative and radical options, on the basis of an appeal to both Scripture and the 'rule of faith' (*regula fidei*). Rather than collapsing the Church into Judaism on the one hand, or allowing a complete divorce on the other, the Fathers proposed a solution that claimed both continuity and discontinuity between the Church and Israel. There is continuity in that the God of Jesus Christ is the creator God of the Scriptures of Israel and Judaism. There is discontinuity in that creation and the Scriptures point beyond themselves to fulfilment in Jesus Christ. This solution represents a considerable achievement in itself. It also makes it worth reiterating that decisions about the place of the Old Testament and the relation between the Testaments are theological and ecclesiological: What kind of God do we believe in? And what kind of people has God called us to be?

## Why has the Old Testament become a problem today?

There are a number of reasons why the reading of the Old Testament is in crisis. One is the widespread 'Marcionite' misconception (reflected in Sir Ian McKellen's attitude reported in Chapter 1) that the God of the Old Testament is a distant, angry, all-powerful father-figure of a rather 'primitive' kind, of whom the least said the better. Far preferable is the gentle, compassionate, loving figure of the Jesus of the Gospels. Indeed, on some versions of this approach, the Jesus of the Gospels is not so much the Son of God the Father as the one who saves us from God the Father! The effect of this is that a wedge is driven between the Old Testament and the New: the Old Testament is a 'problem' because the God of the Old Testament is a problem. In the end, the Old Testament is held in bad odour or becomes dispensable. Its value lies only in showing by how much, in the evolution of religion and the human understanding of God, the Gospel portrayals of Jesus of Nazareth, his life and teaching, supersede the rather crude and brutal God of the Old Testament and the religion of Israel.

A second factor is the subtle but pervasive impact on the Old Testament of historical criticism. Over the past 200 years, a major effort has been made to read and interpret the Old Testament independently of the New and independently of theological, ecclesiastical and liturgical frameworks. This effort has been very successful. It has made possible joint scholarly investigation by Christians and Jews, as well as by scholars of a variety of faiths or none at all. It has also made possible significant historical reconstructions both of the history of Israel and the history of the traditions that make up the Old Testament.

However, the cost of this achievement has been considerable. Its legacy has been to undermine the very considerations that made the Old Testament worthy of attention in the first place – namely, its status and function as part of the Scriptures of two of the world's main religious faith-communities, Jews and Christians. So great is the distance that historical criticism creates between the modern world and the world of ancient Israel that the gulf becomes almost unbridgeable; and instead of life-giving Scripture we are left with ancient sources that are of interest primarily to academic historians. In effect, the Church has been replaced by the scholarly guild, so far as the Bible – especially the Old Testament – is concerned. In other words, necessary historical distancing produced religious alienation: why bother with pre-Christian texts written two or three millennia ago, unless you are interested in antiquity for its own sake?[4]

Ironically, this alienation was sometimes reinforced by religious considerations. That is to say, it was congenial to Protestant historians, predisposed by adherence to the Lutheran principle of 'justification by grace through faith apart from works of the law', to be hostile to Old Testament ideas of law, priesthood and cult – ideas that fell under the damning category of 'works'. The overall effect of this hostility was to render the Old Testament theologically mute. This was achieved by separating as far as possible the Old Testament from the New – the 'legalistic', 'ritualistic' religion of Israel from the 'simple faith' of Jesus, Paul and the early Church.

Third, and not unrelated to the impact of historical criticism on the standing of the Old Testament, has been the success in the natural sciences of evolutionary theory, a success that has spilled over into the social sciences and humanities. In relation to Old Testament interpretation, the tendency has been both to look for evidence of development from simple to more complex social forms and belief systems, and to assume in general that 'old' (as in 'Old Testament') means 'primitive' and therefore dispensable. This assumption has been reinforced massively by the 'science versus creation' debate,[5] in which scientific explanations of the origins of the universe have come, for the most part, to take the place of the myth of creation in the first chapters of Genesis. From the viewpoint of Christian theology and apologetics, a serious mistake was made by those who attempted to refute the scientific proposals on their own (scientific) terms. For the result was, and is, to make the truth claims of Genesis hostage to developments in scientific understanding. Given the success of science in Western culture, this contributes in a powerful way to the continuing disenfranchisement of the Old Testament.

Another reason why the Old Testament has become a 'problem' has to do with certain major cultural trends.[6] One of these is the rise of libertarian individualism in the wake of the Reformation and the Enlightenment. In a libertarian ethos, it is easy to see how the Old Testament, with its focus on personal obedience to Torah and the importance of participation in a cultic society ordered along theocratic lines, could fall into disrepute. Much more attractive, in a culture like this, is the Jesus of the New Testament, since he can be represented as an anti-authoritarian reformer and a hero of the cause of religious and social liberty. On this view, Jesus' contemporaries, the Pharisees and Sadducees, are the heirs of the law-based 'legalistic' religion of Moses and Aaron, while Jesus himself is the radical advocate of love who stands in line with the 'higher religion' of the ethical monotheism taught by the prophets. Thus another wedge is driven between Old Testament and New.

A cultural trend of a not unrelated kind is the trend towards cultural and religious pluralism. In relation to the place of the Bible in society, one result of this pluralism is that the Bible no longer has the iconic quality (as a symbol of Western values and piety) that it once had, since the Bible now has to compete in the market-place of religions with the scriptures of other faiths. Of course, this situation gives rise to new opportunities to commend the Bible and the faith of Christians, but it also contributes to the relativization of the authority of the Bible in Western civilization.

In relation to the Old Testament in particular, one impact of pluralism is that proper sensitivities about respect for Judaism have led to serious questions being asked – by Christians as well as Jews – about the propriety of calling the scriptures of the Jews the 'Old' Testament; for is not such a title, with its implication of something better to come, a slur on the sacred scriptures that Jews call, rather, Hebrew Bible or Torah or Tanakh? And if Christians do not do something about the title 'Old Testament' – replacing it by something like 'First Testament' – are they not contributing to attitudes that in the end may foster anti-semitism? Some argue persuasively that this is indeed so. Others argue that to dispense with the traditional title would be a failure of nerve: the best way to show respect for the differences between the religions of Judaism and Christianity is not to blur or soften them, but to accept that the differences are real – and that goes for their respective scriptures also. For Christians, this means reading the Old Testament as the 'Old', needing to be read in relation to the 'New', *and* reading the New Testament as the 'New', incomprehensible apart from the 'Old'.[7]

A final reason for the crisis surrounding the Old Testament is a failure in Christian practice. At the individual level, the regular reading of the whole Bible as a primary source of inspiration and empowerment for daily living is in serious decline. This decline is only partly restrained by the common practice in some circles of using scriptural selections as a basis for meditation. At the level of corporate liturgical practice (at least in the Church of England), the relatively recent rise to liturgical dominance of the Parish Communion at the expense of the Offices of Morning and Evening Prayer has meant that eucharistic worship has come to predominate over the more Scripture-oriented patterns. This is not to imply that the ASB Communion Service is not scriptural, only that the focus has shifted. In particular, with the placing of the sermon immediately after the Gospel procession and the reading of the Gospel, the tendency is for the first lesson – even when the Old Testament text rather than the New is chosen! – to be marginalized or forgotten. As a result, our familiarity with the Old Testament decreases week by week.

Related to this is a failure in Christian faith and witness, for it is more than likely that the Old Testament has a weak hold on the contemporary Christian imagination because Christians in the relatively affluent West turn to the Bible more for personal consolation than as a springboard for political action and social transformation. It is significant that the recovery of the Old Testament – with its stories of escape from slavery, of the rise and fall of kings and nations, and of prophets protesting against idolatry and injustice in society – is taking place more in the liberation theologies and basic Christian communities of the Third World than in the relatively affluent and secularized churches of the First World. Could it be that we in the West do not read the Old Testament so much because we wish to avoid encounter with that Word of God which, instead of providing consolation, breaks upon us like fire and a hammer (Jeremiah

23.29) and cuts 'like a two-edged sword' (Hebrews 4.12)?

# Why Christians should read the Old Testament (as well as the New)

It is now time to consider positive reasons why the Old Testament is important for Christians.[8] We will then be in a better position to see how we might develop strategies for recovering the Old Testament and strategies for preserving the unity of the Bible as a whole.

The most obvious point is that the Old Testament has been part of the canon of Christian Scripture from earliest times. Therefore the Old Testament is an integral aspect of Christian self-definition, of what it means to be Christian. This pattern of self-definition is not arbitrary either. It is rooted in the Christian memory of the importance of the Jewish Scriptures for Jesus (e.g. Matthew 4.1–11; Mark 10.17–22; Luke 4.16–21; John 5.39–47). It is rooted in the constant appeal to the Jewish Scriptures made by the apostles after Jesus' death and resurrection (e.g. 1 Corinthians 15.3–4; Hebrews 1). It is rooted also in the decisions of the Church Fathers from the second century on to create a single Christian canon incorporating both Testaments.

A second and related reason why we read the Old Testament is that without it the witness of the New Testament writings to Jesus as the Christ of God is incomprehensible. This is so because most, if not all, of the authors of the New Testament were Jews who had come to believe in Jesus as the one in whom the promises of God in Scripture had been fulfilled. So if it was natural for Jesus to think of himself in scriptural terms, it was also just as natural for his first followers to think of him and write about him in scriptural terms.[9]

If, therefore, we wish to understand the testimony of the New Testament to Jesus, we will be unable to do so without a thorough grasp of the story of Israel, as well as of the various ways in which the Jewish Scriptures reflect upon the nature and purposes of God. The most fundamental christological 'titles' that we so often take for granted – Christ (or Messiah), Son of God, Son of Man, Son of David, Lord, Word, Wisdom, and so on – only make sense against the background of Judaism and the Jewish Scriptures.[10] Likewise, the claim that with the coming of Jesus, 'the time is fulfilled, and the kingdom of God is at hand' (Mark 1.15), makes no sense apart from the conception of history as the outworking of the will of God, a conception that comes from the Scriptures of Israel and the Jews.

A third important reason why Christians read the Old Testament is that the Old Testament reveals to us 'the God and Father of our Lord Jesus Christ'. To put it another way, the Old Testament is a fundamental text of Christian theology. In Christian trinitarian faith, it shows us God the Father – the one whose love for the world that he has made culminates in the gift of his Son and the creation of a new people of God enlivened by his Spirit. Without the Old Testament we would not be able to recognize that the revelation given in Jesus Christ is a revelation of God. Nor would we be able to recognize that the story of the Church begins with, and follows on from, the story of Israel. The contribution of the Old Testament is no less vital than that.

Another reason why Christians read the Old Testament has to do with the widespread recognition down the ages of what it adds to the range of scriptural texts available to Christians as a constant source of inspiration, creative reflection and action.[11] Thus for insight into how things are between God and the world, we meditate upon the 'primeval history' of Genesis 1—11. For revelation about who God is and how to live, we read the Pentateuch. For a study in the psychopathology of power, we engross ourselves in the tragedy of King Saul. For insight into the contours of human sin and its repercussions, we follow the story of David and Bathsheba. For a profound meditation on the problem of suffering, we turn to the Book of Job. For words of praise and lament, hope and desolation, blessing and curse, we say the Psalms. For traditional wisdom about human relations and family life, we read Proverbs and Ecclesiastes. To explore the nature of erotic love, there is the poetry of the Song of Songs. In the writings of the prophets, there are words of judgement and mercy to God's people in trouble or gone astray. In the Book of Jonah there is subversive humour and a profound showing of the nature of divine compassion.

The fact that much Old Testament material is strange to modern ears or does not measure up to contemporary moral standards, or is not 'politically correct', does not make it dispensable. What a short-sighted and paternalistic view that is – as if we need to be protected from our own Scriptures! On the contrary, here is what we need to chew on if we are to grow in spiritual maturity. Here is human life unmasked. Here is where our own preconceptions about what is 'obviously the case' are likely to be prised open. Here is where the inextricability of religion, politics and the welfare of society is made undeniably plain. Here is where God and history meet and converse. There is no need, as some claim, to take everything 'literally', as conveying 'what actually happened' or as applying in a straightforward way to how we think and live today. Who would think of 'flattening out' such a wide variety of kinds of texts as are found in the Old Testament so that, in effect, they all end up saying the same thing? Much more worthwhile is the kind of approach that is able to distinguish between what the text says and how God's Spirit may be speaking through it, especially as we read it in worship.

This brings us to one final point about the importance of the Old Testament, which is implicit in what has been said already: its distinctive contribution to Christian worship and spirituality. Through the Christian centuries, this has been true especially perhaps of the Psalms. Bishop Philip Goodrich comments on this in the following terms:

> The Psalms have been described as the necessary roughage for a Christian diet. Opinions vary about their use. Of course they are unparalleled expressions of worship and paeans of praise. They also express profound penitence and deep longing for God: 'Have mercy upon me, O God, after thy great goodness: according to the multitude of thy mercies do away my offences'

36

(Psalm 51). 'Like as the hart desireth the water-brooks; so longeth my soul after thee, O God' (Psalm 42). ... Other people maintain that the enemies which came in for so much rough language in the Psalms are the enemies of the soul, the 'envy, hatred, malice and all uncharitableness', not to mention adulterous thoughts, upon which we must wage continual warfare with a determination to shoot to kill. This also is a valid use of the Psalms. ... Some people speak of the Psalms as borders from which we pluck nosegays along the way. Certainly the Psalms can provide the vocabulary of our prayers. We come before God in silence at the break of day: 'O God, thou art my God: early will I seek thee' (63.1). We are ill or troubled: 'Yea, the darkness is no darkness with thee, but the night is as clear as the day: the darkness and light to thee are both alike' (139.11). We have been let down by friends: 'Yea, even my own familiar friend whom I trusted ... hath laid great wait for me' (41.9); 'O put not your trust in princes nor in any child of man: for there is no help in them' (146.2). ... And of course there are the moments of affirmation: 'O put thy trust in God: for I will yet give him thanks, who is the help of my countenance and my God' (42.15).

(Philip Goodrich, 'The Liturgical Use of Scripture', in John V. Taylor, *et al.*, *Bishops on the Bible* (London, Triangle/SPCK, 1993), pp. 91–3.)

This testimony to some of the ways in which the Psalms 'work' for Christian believers is valid for the Old Testament as a whole. For, in the faith and experience of the Church, the whole of the Old Testament, together with the New, constitute a fount and well-spring for life lived in the grace of God.

## Strategies of recovery

If it is indeed the case, for the kinds of reasons given, that the reading of the Old Testament is in crisis in spite of its historic importance for Christians in all kinds of ways, then it follows that strategies of recovery are needed. One obvious but by no means easy strategy is to resist pressures to marginalize the Old Testament. So, to take up the factors mentioned earlier, if the Old Testament is a problem because the God portrayed there is a problem, then what may be required is a more careful reading of the text. This may reveal that, rather than being a distant, over-bearing father-figure, the fatherly God of the Old Testament is faithful beyond words to his disobedient children, mercifully intervening and rescuing them time and again from the consequences of their waywardness.[12]

Against this backdrop, the story of the Incarnation told in the New Testament should come not as a reversal of the picture of God in the Old Testament, but as its elaboration, its 'fulfilment'. What is more, the Incarnation also provides a crucial theological norm for discriminating, when reading the Old Testament, between what is central and what is peripheral. This allows us to avoid being held to ransom by everything the Old Testament says – as if, from a Christian point of view, some parts are not more important than others.

Taking up another factor, if science has made the Old Testament problematic, then perhaps there are ways of reclaiming the Old Testament. On the one hand, it is important to contest the claims of science to be able to adjudicate on the kinds of truth (about God, history and humankind) revealed in Scripture – since that involves the mistaken claim that science tells us all we can or need to know about the nature of reality.[13] On the other hand, it is equally important not to fight for the authority of the Old Testament on territory to which science lays a legitimate prior claim, as if the Scriptures constitute or contain scientific knowledge of some kind. Whether they do or not is beside the point: which is to resist allowing Scripture to become hostage to science when Scripture's real purpose is to reveal to us the love of God in creation, election and redemption.

The same basic point applies with respect to historical criticism, which is itself but an extension of scientific method into the study of ancient texts like the Bible. If historical criticism has made the Old Testament problematic – by cutting it off from the lifeblood it receives from the faith-communities of Synagogue and Church – then it is important to contest the claim of historical criticism that the historical meaning of the text is its true and only possible meaning, and to urge instead that what the Scriptures mean from the viewpoint of faith is not necessarily given in advance. Historical criticism will certainly contribute to understanding what the text may have meant in its original context (if that can be reconstructed with any plausibility). It will contribute also to an understanding of what effects the text has had and how it has been interpreted down the ages; but it cannot determine what the Old Testament means for communities of faith today. So historical criticism has to be kept in its proper place: to aid us in hearing more clearly than before what God is saying through the Old Testament.[14]

Also to be resisted are those cultural and even religious tendencies that make the Old Testament mute. Secularization, with its hostility to religious tradition, sacerdotal institutions and the authority of sacred texts, is obviously one such tendency. Another is the Western libertarian tradition in its more extreme form – in so far as this tradition neglects an ethic of social responsibility and forgets its historic roots in monotheism. How such all-pervasive forces are to be resisted is, of course, a big question, and one that cannot be tackled here. Suffice it to say that there is now a growing recognition of the wide dimensions of the problem. What is needed in response, perhaps, is the commitment necessary to build patterns of church life of a more counter-cultural kind able to resist more effectively the forces that erode the authority of Scripture. Reclaiming the Old Testament as an essential part of Christian Scripture will be an important step in this direction.

## Towards reading both Testaments as one book

There is, however, one major strategy for recovering the Old Testament that remains to be considered: namely, how better to understand its relation to the New such that the authority of the New Testament for Christian faith is not a constant threat to the authority of the Old. To put it in other words, how best may we read a Bible with two Testaments as one book? This question has attracted renewed interest in recent years, and a useful account is David L. Baker's study, *Two Testaments, One Bible*.[15] His work and that of others shows that there are a number of options, each with its own strengths and weaknesses.

One option, advocated by one of the twentieth century's leading theologians, Rudolf Bultmann, is to conceive of the relationship between Old and New Testaments primarily as one of contrast.[16] The Old Testament is essential as part of the canon, but primarily in a negative way. It is a story of promise unfulfilled, of history miscarrying in such a way that something radically different is required. Theologically and existentially, it is a contrast between law and grace, Israel and the Church. So the Old Testament is the essentially non-Christian presupposition of the New. It reveals the Word of God, but only partially and indirectly since it awaits its fulfilment in the Word-made-flesh. What makes the difference is not that the Old Testament is not also a story of grace, and the New not also a demand for obedience: for grace and law emerge in both. The difference is the radical breaking in of a new, eschatological order of things with the revelation of God in Christ. This revelation is of such a kind that it is impossible to speak of a development in the New of Old Testament ideas of covenant, kingdom of God and people of God: for, in fact, such ideas are completely transformed and human existence comes to be conceived in quite new terms.

This is certainly a formidable position. It stands firmly in line with the Lutheran Reformation tradition with its central focus on the doctrine of justification by faith alone (*sola fide*). It is a bold attempt to interpret theologically the whole of the Bible in the conviction that the God of the Old Testament and the New are one and the same – thus a Marcionite tendency is resisted. It attempts also to give due weight to the fundamental Christian conviction that in Christ the new age has dawned. Furthermore, it provides a theological norm against which the Christian significance of the various parts of Scripture may be judged.

Where it is weak, however, is in its tendency to reduce the biblical claim that God is at work in history (including the history of Israel, Jesus of Nazareth and the Church) to a concern with what the Bible says about the conditions of human existence before and after Christ. That is why the theological categories 'law' and 'gospel' are so crucial for Bultmann. But we may say that while these categories express part of the truth, their effect here is to polarize the two Testaments into the opposition, law *versus* grace, and to shift attention away from the claim of trinitarian faith that the primary subject of the Bible has to do not with the conditions of human existence, but with the revelation in history of God as Father, Son and Holy Spirit.

A second option on the relationship between the Testaments is to view them equally as Christian Scripture.[17] In this century, proponents of this view (albeit in different forms) include Wilhelm Vischer, Karl Barth, George Knight and, most recently, Brevard Childs and Walter Moberly. If we may generalize, their approach is an essentially 'scriptural' one. Both Testaments constitute Christian Scripture, and the theological key to their interpretation is their witness to the redemptive activity of God fulfilled in Christ: the Old Testament tells us *what* Christ is, the New tells us *who* Christ is. Thus, the Old points forward to the New as witness to Christ and the New points back to the Old as its fulfilment. Whereas Bultmann's approach stressed contrast, the emphasis here is on continuity.

This approach is strong for being traditional. It accords with the basic interpretative strategy of the New Testament writers, the Church Fathers and the Reformers, and it is a reading of Scripture in and for the Church. The latter, ecclesial dimension is especially prominent in Childs and Moberly who both stress the normative significance of the early Church's decision to define the canon of Scripture as consisting of both Testaments.[18] This means that Old and New are to be read as equally revelatory of the nature and purposes of God. However, this is not to say that revelation is static and timeless, and that historical consciousness and the results of historical criticism must be pushed aside. Rather, each Testament, read historically and within its canonical context, testifies to God's redemptive activity culminating in Jesus Christ.

This 'scriptural' or 'canonical' approach is still being developed and refined. It has certainly led to a recovery of the idea of the Old Testament as Christian Scripture, in the teeth of powerful forces threatening to divorce completely ('responsible') historical-critical reading in the academy from ('dubious') theological interpretation in the churches. It has contributed also to the recognition that true interpretation of the Bible is a theological enterprise first and foremost. Nevertheless, a number of questions have been raised about its overall viability. One is the question whether this kind of approach hinders truly historical interpretation of the 'Old Testament' as the Scriptures of Israel and the Jews. Another is whether it opens the door to fundamentalist readings of one kind or another which the rise of historical criticism helped to close. Yet another is whether – even if we can agree upon which canon we are talking about (Roman Catholic? Orthodox? Protestant?) – the tendency towards finding points of continuity between the Testaments takes sufficient account of the points of discontinuity both between the Testaments and within each Testament.

A third kind of approach to the relationship between the Testaments, associated especially with the work of the Dutch Reformed scholar Arnold van Ruler, is to turn the first approach virtually on its head by asserting the priority of the Old Testament.[19] On this view, the New Testament remains important – but more in the form of an 'appendix' to the Bible proper. The Old Testament is prior, not only historically but also theologically. For it is there that the God and Father of our Lord Jesus Christ is revealed, and there that the doctrine of the kingdom of God and God's redemptive work in history are set out. The coming of Christ, rather than being the central message of the Bible, is, on this view, more by way of an emergency measure for the sake of the kingdom of God.

What is more, attempts to interpret the Old Testament 'prophetically' as pointing solely to Christ (whether by use of allegory, typology, or whatever) fail to acknowledge not only that this kind of harmonizing of the Testaments neglects the real differences between them, but also that there is a 'surplus' in the Old Testament that christological and spiritualizing interpretations overlook. To put it another way, creation is not there to make possible salvation, but salvation is about the restoration of creation. Similarly, God's dealings with Israel are not merely to prepare the way for the coming of Christ: rather, God's act in Christ is for the benefit of Israel and, through Israel, of all humankind. The business of the Church on this view is not so much to preach Christ (the Lutheran position), but to preach the kingdom of God for the sake of which Christ came.

Van Ruler's position comes as a surprise to Christians the focus of whose faith is the doctrine of the Incarnation – as, classically, in Anglicanism. But it is salutary in many ways: the heavy theological weight that it attributes to the Old Testament; its refusal to collapse the Old Testament into the New; the prominence it gives to the doctrines of God, creation, the kingdom of God and the life of holiness; and its insistence that it is not Christ who is the key to the Old Testament, but the Old Testament that enables us to know what it means to call Jesus 'Christ'. Nevertheless, it may be the case that this approach seriously underestimates what is decisively new in the coming of Christ, so that, from a Christian theological point of view, the priority in reading the two Testaments as one book has to be given to what comes at the end: the revelation of God in Christ crucified and risen.

A fourth way of understanding the relationship between Old and New Testaments that has been influential this century and is associated especially with scholars like Gerhard von Rad, Oscar Cullmann, G. Ernest Wright and Wolfart Pannenberg is the 'salvation history' approach.[20] Fundamental to this view is the claim that the God of Christian faith has revealed himself uniquely in history. The Bible in both Testaments is the proclamation of that history as the history of salvation. This history is a narration of 'the mighty acts of God' which embraces the primeval period, the patriarchs and the history of Israel, and culminates in the Christ-event. The coming of Christ is understood as the historical fulfilment and 'actualization' of all that had gone before.

This approach has obvious strengths. It takes seriously the historical dimension of both Testaments, a dimension that has always been held to be important for traditional Christian faith. It fits also with the theme of promise and fulfilment that runs through the Old Testament and underlies much early Christian thought about how the old dispensation relates to the new. Linked with this is the fact that a salvation history approach does more justice than others, perhaps, to the eschatological dimension of the biblical writings – the sense that the key to the past and the present lies in the future, which is in God's hands. So the hopes of Israel point beyond themselves to something or someone yet to come, and the coming of Christ is the anticipation of a new reality that lies primarily still in the future.

But, as with the other approaches, there are weaknesses and unresolved problems as well. One weakness may be that this approach leaves significant parts of the Old Testament, the less 'historical' parts, out of the frame – the Psalms and the rest of the wisdom literature, in particular. Another has to do with the ambiguity surrounding the term 'salvation history'. What kind of history is this? Is it 'real' history, in the sense of events about which we can have confidence that they actually happened? Or is it history of a different kind, accessible only to the eye of faith or demonstrable only in the light of the end of history (the eschaton)? And which history offers salvation? If it is the reconstructed events behind the text, does the canon of Scripture itself become less important? Furthermore, in the light of more recent attention to the literary qualities of the canon and to interpreting the Bible as literature, some may feel that the salvation history approach fails to do justice to the difference between history and story (or realistic narrative), while also marginalizing the various other literary genres that occur in the canon (like myth, legend, law, poetry, apocalypse, and so on).

## *Conclusion*

A principal value of these and other approaches like them is that they represent serious attempts by Christian scholars to read the Bible as two Testaments, yet one book. They constitute a range of options, none wholly persuasive, that offer creative ways of maintaining the unity of Scripture. They also show that the unity of Scripture is not something that can be drawn in any neat way either from the text of Scripture itself or from the history lying 'behind' the text.

Rather, what we are now in a position to see is that the unity of Scripture is a conceptualization that arises *outside* of Scripture, although in critical dialogue with it. It is a conceptualization that comes from the Church, and represents *a claim of Christian faith* that the entirety of Scripture, the Old Testament and the New, bears authoritative witness in a host of ways to the triune God whom Christians worship.[21] In the final analysis, the insistence that the two Testaments are to be read as one book is a judgement of faith about the authority of Scripture – both as a reliable witness to the oneness of the triune God and as a firm foundation for the unity and catholicity of the Church.

# 4

## The Medium Is The Message?

### or

### The question of Bible genres

## *Introduction*

One of the unique features of the Bible is that although it is a single book (Greek: *biblion*), it contains between its covers many different books (*biblia*). These books, as we have seen in the previous chapter, are themselves separated into two Testaments. They are also, from a literary point of view, books of very different kinds. They vary in literary form or genre: roughly speaking, there is narrative, law, poetry, proverb, parable, prophetic oracle, gospel, epistle, apocalypse – and much more besides.

This means that the witness of the Scriptures to God is *polyphonic*. It speaks with many voices through many different literary media. One of the lasting benefits of historical and literary criticism is that we are more aware of this variety than ever before. The result is that we are able to read the books-within-the-Book with much greater sensitivity, with our hearing much more clearly attuned to the different 'signals' that each book is sending. Put another way, we are less likely now to read the Bible in ways that 'flatten out' the text to the extent that we always find the same message – at least in a superficial sense – wherever we look. We are less likely, that is, to mistake myth or legend for history, poetry for allegory, and prophecy or apocalypse for literal prediction.

Of course, it does not follow that due recognition of the diversity of literary genres in the Bible leads to the conclusion that the witness of the Bible is *incoherent*, the polyphony so great that there is no recognizable harmony. This has been the claim of some critics, especially those determined to interpret the diversity as a form of irredeemable conflict so deep-rooted that any claims about the coherence or unity of Scripture are a case of whistling in the wind. However, we need not deny (as is the tendency in biblical fundamentalism) that this position has some merit and that an intelligible case can be made for it. We need to acknowledge also that those forms of 'biblical theology' that have failed to take the diversity of Scripture sufficiently into account have fallen into disrepute, in some quarters at least.

Nevertheless, there are several reasons for resisting the conclusion that literary diversity in the Bible, together with our increased awareness of the long historical process that shaped the biblical texts, render the final work incoherent. One is the simple observation that, while the Bible may consist of many different literary genres and therefore speak in many different ways, its fundamental subject – the revelation of the triune God – may come through in a way that is not incoherent at all. Another is that, as we saw in the previous chapter, the coherence of the biblical testimony is not just a matter of finding it *in* the text. It is also a matter of bringing it *to* the text in the light of our faith-experience and worship as members of the Church.

Finally, it may be the case that the irreducible diversity of Scripture, both in matters of form and content (and including the 'conflicts' and 'contradictions'), is itself part of the testimony of Scripture: that the God to whom it testifies is a sublime mystery that words are inadequate fully to express. The complex diversity of literary genres in the Bible and the complex history of the traditions that make up the Bible thus become an *invitation* both to forgo premature or simplistic accounts of what the Bible says about who God is, and to contemplate instead the essential mystery to which the texts in all their diversity give access. This access may be limited and partial, but that is necessarily the case given the nature of the mystery that lies at their heart and the frailty of human testimony, however inspired, to the divine. To put it in biblical terms: 'No one has ever seen God' (John 1.18). Though limited, however, the access that

Scripture provides is *sufficient for faith* – and that is all that is required from a Christian point of view.

The aim of this chapter, therefore, is to open up some of the ways in which the diverse literary genres of the Bible contribute to Scripture's primary goal, which is to reveal to us something of the mystery we call God and to bring us to a transforming faith. Since this is obviously a vast subject, what must suffice for our purposes is to take one or two case-studies and work by example. The first will be drawn from narrative material, the second from biblical law.

## 1 Biblical narrative: the story of the Fall (Genesis 3)

Anglican Christians (amongst others) come to the story of the Fall in the context of their preparation for the liturgical season of Advent. Thus, the themes listed in the *Alternative Service Book* for the five Sundays before Advent are: Creation, Fall, Election (Abraham), Promise of Redemption (Moses), and the Remnant of Israel. This liturgical setting is important. It means, on the one hand, that our faith and worship are shaped by a story – not any story, but the particular story that begins where the Bible begins: the creation of a world that is good and that is account-able to the one who made it. But it also means, conversely, that our understanding of the story is shaped by our worship. We do not come to it 'cold'; rather, the story of creation and fall are part of a much larger liturgical action in which we celebrate God's coming to us in his Son in judgement (Advent) and mercy (Christmas).

Such considerations are not incidental. The fact that our faith and worship are story-shaped gives a vital *particularity* to all that we say and do as a Christian community. What is more, the story that begins with creation, fall, the call of Abraham, and so on, gives our faith and worship a rootedness in the reality of human creatureliness in time and space. This implies that our faith and worship are not understood as flights of fancy, even though the stories are profound works of the religious imagination. It implies also that, even if they are not adequate as scientific or historical accounts of the origins of the universe or the history of Israel, they may nevertheless be held to be true – as an account in narrative form and in the genre we call 'myth' of what is 'really real' about the nature of reality and what it means to be human in the light of that reality.[1]

If we ask how they may be held to be true as stories about what is 'really real', the answer we can give comes in turn from our faith and worship. The stories on their own do not speak for themselves; nor does it do much good to try to harness science or history to speak for them, since what usually happens is that, in the end, science and history cannot be found to speak with any clarity one way or the other – due to the fact that they are not qualified to do so – or that science and history drown out what the stories themselves are trying to reveal. Rather, just as the stories shape our faith and worship, so our faith and worship prove in a 'deep-down' sense the truth of the stories: that the world is the good creation of a God who is gracious, that humankind is made in the image of God, that humankind threatens repeatedly to unmake because of sin what God has made, and that God does not give up in his love for the world.

To understand the story of the Fall, we need to start at the beginning, with the story of creation, in chapters 1 and 2 of Genesis.[2] These chapters express, in a very simple but profound narrative, the greatness of God and the priority of grace. Christians do believe in 'original sin', but they believe even more in 'original grace': for the Fall takes place after the creation and therefore within the larger purposes of God's creative power. In Genesis 1.1—2.4, God shows his greatness by marvellous acts of creativity in which the universe is brought into being and order is brought out of chaos. Significant is the way in which creation proceeds by divine acts of distinction and separation that make life possible, and that are deemed each time to be 'good': the light is separated from the darkness, heaven from earth, the waters from the dry land, the sun by day from the moon by night, the air and water creatures from the land creatures, and male humanity from female. The final – and therefore most significant – act of separation is the setting apart of the sabbath day from the other six. For what we are meant to see is that, in the ordering of the acts of creation, there is a very particular end in view: namely, that of all created things sharing in the divine life, which is characterized as 'rest'. So the story of creation is one of God's life-giving grace from beginning to end.

In Genesis 2.4b–25, the creation story is told from a different perspective. Instead of acts of distinction, there is a forging of bonds: between the human and the soil, the human and animals, and the man and the woman. Just as the first creation account ends on the high note of God 'blessing' the seventh day, so too the second account ends on a high note of blessing, in the mutual delight of the man and the woman: 'And the man and his wife were both naked, and were not ashamed' (2.25).

So our story as a whole begins with a sequence of divine words and acts that show the grace of God and the goodness of all that God has made. This implies that whatever happens after this happens within this framework: that God is over all, God's creation is good, and God's grace is the reality undergirding all else. This is important for Christian faith. In particular, it serves to counteract powerful tendencies that the stories following the creation story might be seen to encourage: towards all-pervasive pessimism about what it means to be human; or towards hostility to the material world; or towards idolatrous behaviour that mistakes what is creaturely for the heavenly creator.

This brings us to the story of the Fall, in Genesis 3.[3] If Genesis 1—2 is about creation, much of what follows in Genesis 3—11 is about uncreation, the undoing of all the good that God has done, with a return to chaos a real possibility. In other words, if Genesis 1—2 is about the spread of grace, Genesis 3—11 looks to be about the spread of sin. So, in the sequence of the narrative, we move from the disobedience of Adam and Eve in the garden, to Cain's fratricide (4.1–16), a reckless killing by Lamech (4.23–4), the titanic lust of 'the sons of God' for 'the daughters of men' (6.1–4), the total corruption in the generation of the Flood (6.5ff), and, finally, the hubris of the builders of the tower of Babel (11.1–9). It is as if the narrator is wanting to say that, tragically, sin is an inescapable element of the human condition (which is what is meant by the doctrine of 'original sin'), and that the life made possible by God is always vulnerable to the waywardness of human beings.

The first episode in this catalogue of disasters is especially significant, however, because it is paradigmatic of all the rest: which is why it has become known as the story of 'the Fall'. To understand it better, we need to analyse the story in more detail. The first thing to note is that Adam and Eve are *representative* figures. 'Adam' means not man as male, but man as human being (or 'earth creature', there being a pun between the Hebrew words *adam* and *adamah*, which means 'earth'). So the story is not about two historical characters, Adam and Eve, but about two representative human beings, Everyman and Everywoman; and what we have in Genesis 1—3 is the kind of religious language we call 'myth', which is the type of language we need to use to talk about the true nature of the human situation.

A second point is that the story in Genesis presupposes what happens in 2.15–17. Here, God puts man in the garden to look after it. So man is given responsibility and the dignity that goes with it. He is also given a command that, while it includes the prohibition not to eat of the fruit of one particular tree, is noteworthy more for the freedom it allows: 'You may freely eat of every tree of the garden ...' (2.16). The implication of the prohibition is not that God is a mean tyrant, but that God is doing something for man's good by preserving an essential distance between the creature and the creator. In sum, the main elements are: the dignity accorded man by giving him responsibility in the garden of God, the fact that this responsibility involves living according to God's command (so it is a freedom within limits), and the warning that choosing to disobey leads to what is called 'death'.

Now notice that, in blatant contradiction to what we have just discovered, the first words of the serpent (who appears on the scene, unexplained, in 3.1ff) imply that God is not interested in doing the best for man by allowing him responsible freedom, but rather is out to deny Adam and Eve what is rightfully theirs.

We have here a masterly exploration of the psychology of temptation. God had said, 'You may freely eat of every tree of the garden …'. But the serpent twists this right around in the question, 'Did God say, "You shall not eat of any tree of the garden"?' (3.1). The serpent then goes on to deny that they will die if they eat the forbidden fruit, and claims instead that good will result: they will see things in a new way and, even more tempting, they will be 'like God, knowing good and evil' (3.5). So what happens subsequently is a way of showing how disastrous it is to disobey the will of the creator God, in spite of the apparent attractiveness of doing so.

The woman eats and the man eats also. They act together: so both share full responsibility. In spite of the way in which an early Christian tradition like 1 Timothy 2.14 places primary blame upon the woman and exculpates the man, the thrust of the narrative proper is on the shared responsibility and culpability of both the man and the woman; and the narrative oscillates back and forth, giving first one the initiative and then the other. The line taken in 1 Timothy can hardly be normative. Not only does it reflect to a large degree the sexual politics of the early Church (in which the aim of the leaders was to preserve order by suppressing innovation in gender roles), it also, ironically, mirrors the buck-passing stance adopted by the man when interrogated by God: 'The woman whom thou gavest to be with me, she gave me fruit of the tree, and I ate' (3.12)![4]

Then comes a surprise. What God threatened ('you shall surely die') does not seem to happen. Instead, what the serpent promises does happen! Their eyes are opened (3.7), and they do indeed become like God, knowing good and evil (3.22a). Or is the surprise meant as an encouragement to look at a deeper level for the working out of the penalty? In fact, 'death' does begin to manifest itself. The man and the woman hide from the presence of God which they had enjoyed with such intimacy beforehand (3.8). The man testifies to his fear at the sound of God in the garden (3.10). Relationships begin to break down: the man blames both the woman and God (3.12); and the woman blames the serpent (3.13).

In other words, all the good created by God begins to turn to uncreation, between God and humankind, the man and the woman, and humankind and the animals. And this breakdown leads to further breakdown: the serpent becomes subject to a curse (3.14–15); woman's honoured roles as wife and child-bearer become subject, respectively, to domination and pain (3.16); man's role as tiller of the soil becomes subject to hardship and curse, and his end will be an ignominious return to the dust (3.17–19); and, to cap it all, they are expelled from the garden and therefore, from the presence of God and the tree of life (3.22–4). A catalogue of curse and woe like this speaks very plainly of the catastrophic consequences that the story-teller believes follow inevitably from disregarding God's will and from every human attempt to become 'like God', judging for ourselves instead of letting God be judge.

This sombre note is the one on which the story of the Fall ends. It is the sombre understanding of the human condition which Christian faith down the ages has found to be true. That is why hearing the story in the period of preparation for Advent is so appropriate. Adam and Eve are indeed Everyman and Everywoman. Their story is also our story; and the liturgical calendar makes it possible for us to make that discovery year after year. Of course, the Fall is not the end of the story. Even within the story there are hints that all is not lost. The man bestows a name on the woman, calling her 'Eve', in recognition of the fact that 'she was the mother of all living' (3.20); and God makes skin clothing for them (3.21) – a considerable improvement on the aprons of fig leaves they had made earlier for themselves (cf. 3.7)! Even the expulsion from the garden is an act of mercy since it means that, cut off from the tree of life (3.24), their days of pain and toil will not go on indefinitely.

St Paul was right in affirming that 'all have sinned and fall short of the glory of God' (Romans 3.23), but what Paul expresses in the succinct, propositional language of his letter, Genesis presents in the extended narrative form of myth. As we have been able to see, it is the peculiar advantage of this narrative form that it is able to lay things out before us in ways that *engage our imaginations* as well as our intellects. It also enables, in ways quite personal and vivid, the subtle exploration of the nature of the human condition, of God, grace, creatureliness, temptation, sin, and so on, which more formal, propositional language does not.

What is more, there is in the narrative form in Genesis an 'open' quality and a *surplus of meaning* which invite more than one reading. It is as if we are being teased by the story into return visits for further reflection on what it is about. Is it a 'fall' story only or is it a story of growth to painful maturity? Why does God allow the serpent to be in the garden in the first place? Why is the theme of the nakedness of the man and the woman given so much attention? Is the woman especially to blame or not and, if not, why has the story been interpreted that way so often down the ages? What is meant by 'the tree of the knowledge of good and evil', and why is the fruit of that tree prohibited? What is 'the tree of life', and what is meant by 'life' and 'death' in the story?

We would not be so likely to be enticed into asking these kinds of questions faced with the proposition of Paul, that 'all have sinned and fall short of the glory of God'. This is not to deny the importance either of what Paul says or of propositional language in theology. Rather, it is to make the point that the biblical narrative of Genesis speaks in a way that has its own unique, irreplaceable effect precisely because of its form *as narrative*. It may even be the case that no other literary form is as appropriate as narrative to bring home to us as readers and hearers the profound mysteries at the heart of reality that are opened up in Genesis 1—3.

## 2  Biblical law: keeping the sabbath

If much of the Bible comes to us in the form of narrative, much of the Bible also comes to us in the form of law or command-ment or instruction. In addition, the subject of the law – its status, what it is for, how it is to be obeyed, who is to enforce it, and so on – runs through the Bible as a whole. Indeed, if we look

at the Bible as one book made up of two Testaments, it is striking that law comes at the beginning of both: in the Old
Testament, it comes in the Pentateuch (the first five books,
traditionally ascribed to Moses the law-giver), and in the New
Testament, it comes in the Gospel of Matthew – above all, in the
Sermon on the Mount (Matthew 5—7, noting especially
5.17–20). So law is a characteristic of the biblical literature both
in terms of genre and of subject-matter.[5]

What is it, then, that makes biblical law so important? This is
a question worth asking, not least because from Jesus and Paul
on, the law has been a subject of enormous controversy in the
Christian Church, with the consequence that sometimes biblical
law has fallen into disrepute. This has happened for various
reasons: Jesus got into trouble with the Pharisees over it; Paul
taught that salvation was by faith in Christ, not 'works of the law';
to the increasingly Gentile Church the law was irrelevant or an
anachronism unless interpreted allegorically; Marcion and the
Gnostics wanted to dispense with it and to cut Christianity off
from its Jewish roots altogether; the Protestant Reformation cast
the Roman Catholic Church in the mould of a legalistic religion
from which the preaching of the righteousness of Christ was the
only possible escape; for the Puritans, and subsequently in
Victorian times, observance of the Commandments – especially
observance of the Lord's Day – became a focus of religious identity; and, in the present cultural climate, the emphasis on
individual choice and moral freedom militates against sympathy
towards religions advocating discipline and moral rigour. And
this summary of factors only scratches the surface of things!

So a good case can be made for looking again at biblical law,
not only because it is one of the key types of literature in the
Bible, but also because history shows that a lot is at stake theologically, religiously and culturally. What is important for our
purposes is to explore, in an introductory way, what biblical law
has to offer. In order to do this we will focus on one aspect of
law: the teaching about the sabbath.

But before we do, we need to try to answer our earlier question: why is biblical law important – that is to say, why is it

important as one of the most significant media of revelation in biblical literature? Why is law important *in its form as law*? One clue to the answer is that, in the paradigmatic case of the Ten Commandments, it is God who speaks them, and he speaks them directly to all the people, not just to an elite (Exodus 20.1). In addition, it is noticeable that most of the Commandments are prohibitions: 'You shall not ...'. In other words, they establish certain clear boundaries without being very specific on how life is to be conducted within those boundaries. So as well as a certain element of restriction, there is very significant scope for freedom. What these observations imply is that the Commandments are a very direct expression of the *personal relationship* between God and his people, a relationship that is loving and life-giving. Having rescued them from slavery in Egypt and brought them across the Red Sea, God now gives them basic rules to live by in order that they might continue to be in relationship with him.

Not all biblical laws are of this direct 'You shall not' kind (which scholars call 'apodeictic'). Others are of the 'if such-and-such happens, then do so-and-so' kind (which scholars call 'casuistic' law or case-law). But the main point holds good: that biblical law expresses in a way much more direct and economical than in narrative that God is with his people and that God's care for his chosen people is so strong that he does not leave them without clear parameters within which they will prosper and find life. Thus, it is by no means coincidental that, following the death of the law-giver Moses and at the point where Joshua assumes the leadership of Israel, what is stressed is the importance for success of continual meditation upon 'the book of the law' (Joshua 1.7–9):

> Only be strong and very courageous, being careful to do according to all the law which Moses my servant commanded you; turn not from it to the right hand or to the left, that you may have good success wherever you go. This book of the law shall not depart out of your mouth, but you shall meditate on it day and night, that you may

be careful to do according to all that is written in it; for then you shall make your way prosperous, and then you shall have good success. Have I not commanded you? Be strong and of good courage; be not frightened, neither be dismayed; for the LORD your God is with you wherever you go.

This main point about biblical law is reinforced by a further consideration. This is that the basic Hebrew term *torah* means more than 'law' in the narrow sense of particular laws. The basic sense of *torah* is 'instruction' or 'teaching'. This broader understanding is reflected in the fact that the whole of the first five books of the Bible came to be known as Torah. Since the Torah is an account of Israel's rescue and election by God to be his special people, the instructions or commandments God gives are clearly meant to be direct expressions of that relationship, given for the people's good. To grasp this is crucial, because it both makes it possible to see what particular laws are for, and it guards against the common confusion between law and 'legalism'. The two are not the same. Law or *torah* is a form of divine revelation showing how God's people are to live for him: legalism is the following of laws for their own sake, as an alternative to following them for God's sake. The common accusation that the religion of Israel or of the Jews is a 'legalistic' religion – an accusation that Christians not infrequently address also to fellow-Christians! – usually reflects a serious failure on the part of the accuser to appreciate that the sign of true devotion to God is deliberate and thorough-going personal obedience in every area of life.[6]

Turning now to biblical law concerning *the sabbath*, it is important to note that sabbath observance is a weighty matter in the Bible as a whole. It is especially so in the Old Testament, where it has particular prominence both as the climax of the story of creation (Genesis 2.2–3), and as the fourth of the Ten Commandments (Exodus 20.8–11; Deuteronomy 5.12–15). But we know as well that Jesus observed the sabbath, even if it is clear that his priorities in doing so differed from those of his co-religionists, the Pharisees (cf. Mark 2.23—3.6; John 5.9–18). Paul himself probably observed the sabbath, as a way of maintaining his links with the synagogue communities; but, in contrast to fellow Jewish Christians, he refused to make sabbath observance binding on Gentile Christians (cf. Galatians 4.8–11; Romans 14.1–9; Colossians 2.16–17).

Gradually, observance of 'the Lord's Day' (the first day of the week) became standard Christian practice (cf. 1 Corinthians 16.2; Acts 20.7; Revelation 1.10), and the Fourth Commandment was reinterpreted to apply to that day instead. For present-day Christians, it is generally understood in historical terms as one of the roots in Judaism of the Christian Sunday – but some, like the Seventh Day Adventists, continue to observe the sabbath day itself. In recent years in Britain, sabbath law has come to life again in the context of the political debate over the deregulation of Sunday trading and the spirited opposition mounted by the 'Keep Sunday Special' campaign. So we are not talking about a commandment on the periphery. It is weighty in biblical terms, and for both Jews and Christians today it has very considerable continuing significance.[7]

To understand it better, though, we need to turn to the text of the Ten Commandments (Exodus 20.1–17; Deuteronomy 5.1–21). A number of general points are worth making at the start. First, the sabbath is one of ten 'words': 'And God spoke all these *words*, saying ...' (Exodus 20.1; cf. Deuteronomy 4.13; 10.4). So even though we call them 'commandments', they are perhaps more truly thought of as revelation. This helps to counteract any pejorative sense that words like 'commandment' or 'law' might have. It also makes sense of the fact that the first 'word' begins in a way that does not sound like commandment or law at all: 'I am the LORD your God, who brought you out of the land of Egypt, out of the house of bondage ...' (Exodus 20.2). The fourth 'word', about the sabbath, should also therefore be thought of in this light. The teaching about the sabbath is a part of God's rescuing a people to live for him in his presence. The sabbath 'word' is another act of divine grace intended to further the liberation of the people of God.

Second, this 'word' about the sabbath has been carefully prepared for, and comes as no surprise. Prior to the revelation at Sinai, the commandment to observe the sabbath comes in the story of the manna in the wilderness, in Exodus 16 (especially vv. 22–30), an episode intended to show that resting on the sabbath is an act of faith in God – that God will 'give us each day [even the day on which we refrain from work] our daily bread'. The fact that God does supply sufficient manna to carry the people through the sabbath prepares the way for the sabbath commandment by showing that God is trustworthy and the sabbath is for the people's good.

Even more significant preparation for the 'word' on the sabbath, however, is the story of creation, where the climax of God's creative acts is to rest on the seventh day (Genesis 2.2–3)! This correspondence between the story of creation and the story of Israel's election implies that there is an essential correspondence between who God is and what kind of people Israel is to be. As God rested, so too Israel is to rest; and the act of observing the sabbath is an important way to honour God and to share in the life of God. The fact that the seventh day is the first thing in creation that God pronounces 'holy' (2.3), not only testifies to the significance of the sabbath, but also implies that observing the sabbath is a way of sharing that holiness. The eminent Jewish scholar Abraham Heschel makes the point with lyrical beauty:

> One of the most distinguished words in the Bible is the word *qadosh*, holy; a word which more than any other is representative of the mystery and majesty of the divine. Now what was the first holy object in the history of the world? Was it a mountain? Was it an altar? It is, indeed, a unique occasion at which the distinguished word *qadosh* is used for the first time: in the Book of Genesis at the end of the story of creation. How extremely significant is the fact that it is applied to time: 'And God blessed the seventh *day* and made it *holy*.' ... He who wants to enter the holiness of the day must first lay down the profanity

of clattering commerce, of being yoked to toil. He must go away from the screech of dissonant days, from the nervousness and fury of acquisitiveness and the betrayal in embezzling his own life. He must say farewell to manual work and learn to understand that the world has already been created and will survive without the help of man. Six days a week we wrestle with the world, wringing profit from the earth; on the Sabbath we especially care for the seed of eternity planted in the soul. ... The Sabbath is a day for the sake of life. Man is not a beast of burden, and the Sabbath is not for the purpose of enhancing the efficiency of his work. ... The Sabbath is not for the sake of the weekdays; the weekdays are for the sake of the Sabbath. It is not an interlude but the climax of living.
(Abraham Heschel, *The Sabbath: Its Meaning for Modern Man* (New York, Noonday Press, 1990), pp. 9, 13–14.)

We are now in a good position to consider the 'word' about the sabbath in more detail. It comes in two versions, set out below:

Remember the sabbath day, to keep it holy. Six days you shall labour, and do all your work; but the seventh is a sabbath to the LORD your God; in it you shall not do any work, you, or your son, or your daughter, your manservant, or your maidservant, or your cattle, or the sojourner who is within your gates; for in six days the LORD made heaven and earth, the sea, and all that is in them, and rested the seventh day; therefore the LORD blessed the sabbath day and hallowed it. (Exodus 20.8–11)

Observe the sabbath day, to keep it holy, as the LORD your God commanded you. Six days you shall labour and do all your work; but the seventh day is a sabbath to the LORD your God; in it you shall not do any work, you, or your son, or your daughter, or your manservant, or your maidservant, or your ox, or your ass, or any of your cattle, or the sojourner who is within your gates, that your manservant and your maidservant may rest as well as you. You shall remember that you were a servant in the land of Egypt, and the LORD your God brought you out thence with a mighty hand and an outstretched arm; therefore the LORD your God commanded you to keep the sabbath day. (Deuteronomy 5.12–15)

The location of this 'word' at a pivotal point in the sequence of the ten 'words' is significant. It links together the 'vertical' commandments about how to relate truly to God and the 'horizontal' commandments about how to relate truly to one's neighbour. This is because the sabbath commandment combines both elements. It is about sharing in the rest ordained by God in creation, keeping that day separate (or 'holy') for God; and it is about allowing one's fellow creatures to share in that rest as well.

Also striking is the amount of attention devoted to the sabbath. Unlike most of those that follow, the sabbath law is extensive. But the elaboration focuses not on detailed instruction about how to keep the sabbath, but on who should share in its blessings and why it should be kept. The one prohibition – and there is only one – is that no work should be done – but, even then, what constitutes 'work' is left unspecified! Once again we are forced to acknowledge that this 'word' or law is not meant to be burdensome. There is no 'kill-joy' mentality here. Rather, it is intended to *make space* for the free enjoyment of the best things in life. The boundaries that create this space are the temporal boundary ('Remember the sabbath day') and the disciplinary boundary ('in it you shall not do any work').

A comparison of the two forms of this commandment shows that the formulation is rather fluid. This is indicative of the general point that there is a sense in which (ironically) the Ten Commandments are *not* 'written in stone'! The basic teaching is the same, certainly; but there is evidence of development and adaptation as well. For the whole point of the Commandments is to be life-giving to God's chosen people: so changes in the circumstances of the people or developments in understanding are reflected in modifications of the Commandments. Also, from the point of view of the Christian canon, having this commandment in two forms not only reinforces by repetition what they have in common, but also allows the commandment to be appreciated in more than one way.

Interestingly, the shorter form in Exodus 20 gives a rationale for sabbath-keeping drawn from the story of creation: 'for in six days the LORD made heaven and earth, the sea, and all that is in them, and rested the seventh day ...' (20.11). This implies that by keeping the sabbath, Israel participates in the imitation of God and experiences a kind of return to the garden of Eden! Heschel captures this aspect beautifully:

> To observe the Sabbath is to celebrate the coronation of a day in the spiritual wonderland of time, the air of which we inhale when we 'call it a delight'. Call the Sabbath a delight [Isaiah 58.13]: a delight to the soul and a delight to the body. ... 'Sanctify the Sabbath by choice meals, by beautiful garments; delight your soul with pleasure and I will reward you for this very pleasure' [Deuteronomy rabba 3,1].'
> (Abraham Heschel, *The Sabbath: Its Meaning for Modern Man* (New York, Noonday Press, 1990), pp. 18–19.)

The longer form in Deuteronomy 5 gives a different, though by no means incompatible rationale to do with the imperative of social justice ('that your manservant and your maidservant may rest *as well as you*'), in the light of Israel's experience of rescue from slavery in Egypt. Once again it is a matter of the imitation of God: God's people are to act towards each other and their neighbours as God has acted towards them. It is worth noting, especially in the light of our ecological concerns at the end of the twentieth century, that 'neighbours' (in both versions, but elaborated significantly in Deuteronomy) includes domestic animals: 'your ox, or your ass, or any of your cattle' (Deuteronomy 5.14). They are to share in the sabbath rest as well – another touch of the symbolism of Eden, perhaps?

In sum, putting the two together allows us to see why the sabbath commandment ('word') is so important. The sabbath makes possible the imitation of God and therefore a sharing in the life of God. This is a sharing both in God as the creator and in God as the redeemer and liberator. What makes this sharing possible is obedience to the bench-mark prohibition, 'you shall not do any work'. This creates the boundary – the *wide* boundary – within which God's people are free to share in God's good gifts.

## Conclusion

The Bible consists of many books which themselves contain a wide variety of literary forms. We have looked at only two – narrative and law – but we have seen that these are not insignificant examples! Not only do these two forms take up a good proportion of the Bible as a whole, but they also illustrate well the fact that the different types of literature allow the Bible to 'speak' in different ways. Thus whereas narrative engages us at the level of the imagination, law engages us at the level of the will.

A similar case could be made for other biblical genres also.[8] So it might be said that the Psalms engage our emotions, the Song of Songs our desire, the wisdom literature our intellect, apocalyptic our intuitions or dreams, and so on. Of the Gospels, it might even be said that there is a sense in which they engage us at all of these levels: both because they contain in a concentrated way many of the literary forms found scattered elsewhere in the Bible, and because their subject is too rich to be expressible in one or two forms only. If this is true of the Gospels, it is true on a wider scale of the Bible as a whole. For, in the faith of Christians nurtured by worship, it is the very polyphony of the Bible that allows it to function as revelation of the mystery of God.

# 5

## Why Four Gospels?

### or
### Will the 'car accident' analogy do?

## *Introduction*

The presence in the canon of Christian Scripture of four Gospels rather than one is among its most striking features.[1] Sometimes this feature is ignored on the assumption that they all really say the same thing. Of course, there may be something in this. To discover what it is that all four Gospels 'really say', we could turn quite properly to the creeds of the Church, since it is the creeds that are the Church's attempt to give a normative account of the gospel in the Gospels. On the other hand, the problem is that it is quite easy also to show on another level that the Gospels do not say the same thing! Instead, they differ quite significantly both in points of detail and on a larger scale as well. We shall see this both in our case study in this chapter, and in our encounter with the Gospel of John in the next.

Sometimes the fact that there are four Gospels is seen as an advantage. The common analogy is quasi-judicial: that of witnesses of a car accident testifying in court to what they have seen. As this analogy goes, the more witnesses there are, the stronger are our chances of determining what actually happened, and the differences between the various testimonies are best explained as due to the different standpoints from which the accident was observed. Once again, this kind of approach has something to commend it. We do feel more confident about the witness of the first followers of Jesus about him when we know we have the independent testimony of more than one of them.

But there are problems here too. The various accounts may be so different as to cast serious doubt on the possibility of ever knowing what actually happened. What is more, such differences may make us question whether the 'car accident' analogy is a very good one for understanding what the Gospel writers are trying to do. Are they trying to give an 'objective' account of 'what actually happened', or are they trying to persuade their readers of something very difficult to put into words: that in Jesus, God has come near and calls us to follow in faith?[2] Is our tendency to think of truth primarily on the model of what can be proven by appeal to witnesses in a court of law (what a friend of mine refers to as 'Old Bailey theology'!) adequate to the task of testing out the kind of truth to which the Gospels testify?

This raises straight away the question: What is a Gospel? In our kind of culture with its roots in British empiricism and Enlightenment rationalism, there is a common tendency to answer this question with a simple alternative: a Gospel is either a factual reporting of events about Jesus or it is a fictional representation. The assumption lying beneath this set of alternatives is that facts are what count, not fiction, and that public truth has to do with observable facts, while fiction (or legend, or myth, or religion) is a matter of private values and personal preference. Once this polarization is accepted, the tendency of readers of the Gospels is either to argue as hard as possible for their factual accuracy in order to defend their credibility, or to dismiss the Gospels as fiction and thereby to marginalize the truth-testimony they offer. On both sides, there is the tendency towards what has been called a '100 per cent mentality'. Either the Gospels are completely accurate historically and therefore true, or they are inaccurate historically and therefore false.

But what if the Gospels resist this kind of polarization? What if they are neither 'fact' nor 'fiction', neither 'history' nor 'myth'? What if the truth of the Gospels is something more profound than the question of their historical accuracy? Is the reason why the Christian canon contains four Gospels, all with as many differences as similarities, *an invitation to see (and read) them in another way*? This is why an increasing number of interpreters of the Bible are coming to see the Gospels in more complex terms as testimonies to Christ in narrative form – testimonies that proclaim in narrative Christ as God's 'good news' for all creation, and that differ because the reality to which they testify cannot be contained in any single, 'objective' account.[3]

## *Jesus in Gethsemane*

In order to illustrate this point, it is best if we look at a particular case-study. The one I have chosen is the powerful and well-known story of Jesus in Gethsemane.[4] It comes clearly in three versions in the Gospels of Matthew, Mark and Luke. In the Gospel of John the story is transformed into something quite different. There may be also another allusion to the episode, in the Epistle to the Hebrews, where the writer says: 'In the days of his flesh, Jesus offered up prayers and supplications, with loud cries and tears, to him who was able to save him from death, and he was heard for his godly fear' (Hebrews 5.7). But we cannot go into that text here.

If we concentrate on the accounts in the Gospels, we realize very quickly that, while the broad contours are clear enough, it is impossible to make a detailed reconstruction of what actually happened. For example, there is the problem of deciding the original text in Luke's version, where the most ancient manuscripts omit verses 43–4 (which speak of the angel appearing and of Jesus' sweat dropping like blood as he prays). Then there are other questions. Did Jesus pray three times (so Mark and Matthew) or once (so Luke)? Did he take Peter, James and John with him (so Mark and Matthew) or not (so Luke)? What words did Jesus actually say? Why is John's account so different that the tradition about Jesus' prayer in Gethsemane immediately prior to his arrest is all but obliterated? In any case, was it Gethsemane, and was it a garden? Only Mark and Matthew locate the event in Gethsemane, Luke refers more generally to the Mount of Olives; and it is only John where mention is made of a garden, which is situated 'across the Kidron Valley' (John 18.1).

Such differences cannot be denied. Nor are they explained away convincingly by appeal to some version of the 'car accident' hypothesis referred to above – particularly as, in this case, three of the key witnesses (or all of them, if we follow Luke) are reported to have fallen asleep at the crucial point! What we have here is not eyewitness reporting direct from the spot, but four carefully constructed *narratives*. There is no need to deny that early tradition based on the testimony of eyewitnesses lies behind these narratives, since it is very hard to think of convincing reasons why the followers of Jesus might want to fabricate a story of this kind which (it could be argued) shows Jesus in such a weak light. But that is different from claiming that the accounts of Jesus in Gethsemane are 'straight history' and tell us 'what actually happened'. Far more consistent with the nature of the material itself is the recognition that what we are dealing with is neither 'brute fact' nor 'irrelevant fiction', but historically grounded narrative written (as we shall see) *from faith for faith*.

What does this insight mean for how the various Gospel accounts are to be read? The main point about method is that, instead of using the Gospel texts *as sources* to reconstruct what we can then claim to be the 'really real' historical event lying behind the text, we attend as carefully as we can to the text *as text* and try to discern what the writers are trying to say in their versions of the story. To put it another way, the difference is between *using* the text (for historical reconstruction) and *listening* to the text (as 'good news' from God). The advantage of the latter approach is that it is more consistent both with the type of literature a Gospel is – namely, Christian proclamation in the form of what the ancients would have recognized as biography[5] – and with the kinds of personal and social transformation the Gospels are trying to make possible.

Another advantage of this approach is that differences between the various Gospel accounts are not automatically interpreted as a problem or a threat, as if there is one, single, true interpretation (the one to do with 'what actually happened') which any hint of 'contradiction' will throw into doubt. On the contrary, by listening trustfully to these narratives, we come to recognize in the differences between them (as well as in what they have in common) invitations to consider from more than one perspective the meaning and truth of what is told. After all, if the Gospels are testimonies to a truth that is inexhaustible and to a mystery that is unfathomable, would we not be more surprised if they all saw things the same way?

MARK'S NARRATIVE

Mark's narrative of Jesus in Gethsemane is very powerfully told. Jesus has shared a last Passover meal and sung a hymn with his disciples, and they go out of the city to the Mount of Olives. There, in the imagery of shepherd and sheep from Zechariah, Jesus prophesies the coming catastrophe and contradicts Peter's protestations of loyalty by prophesying his threefold denial (14.26–31). It is as if the darkness that covers the earth at the crucifixion (15.33) is beginning to fall already, and Jesus alone can see it coming.

So he needs to pray. He has prayed before according to Mark's narrative (e.g. 1.35–9; 6.46) and he has instructed his disciples about the importance of prayer, especially in times of confrontation with the powers of darkness (9.28–9).[6] And now prayer is more important than ever, for 'the hour' of his death has come. As if to emphasize that this is a crisis in Jesus' life like no other, it is worth noting that whereas earlier Jesus prays on his own, now he desires the company of his friends (14.33). Nor does he conceal his true feelings, either from his friends (14.33–4) or from God (14.36). Jesus shrinks from the suffering and death that awaits him. To the disciples he says that his soul is sorrowful, 'even to death'. To God he prays, 'remove this cup from me' – the cup being a biblical symbol of suffering inflicted as a punishment for sin.

Jesus' prayer in Gethsemane, like Jacob at the Jabbok, is a wrestling with God: and there are no short-cuts, no evasions, no denials. Jesus prays not once, but three times. Each time, the prayer is the same (14.39). The repetition is not for repetition's sake or as if God has not heard the first time. Rather, it conveys

Jesus' persistent faithfulness to the God whom he is able to call 'Abba, Father'. It speaks also of Jesus' deepening acceptance of his death as the way God has chosen for him: his complete and final alignment of his will with the will of God. Jesus, ever the teacher careful for the instruction of his followers, himself provides the commentary on his praying: 'Watch and pray that you may not enter into temptation; the spirit indeed is willing, but the flesh is weak' (14.38). By the end of the episode, Jesus shows that he himself has remained faithful to his calling. As he has overcome temptation at the beginning of his work (1.12–13), now he overcomes it again at the point of its aweful culmination, and is able to go forward to meet his betrayer (14.42).

But if Mark's narrative highlights Jesus' faithful sonship in coming through prayer to bring his will into alignment with the will of the Father, it highlights also the faithlessness of the disciples. The privileged trio, Peter, James and John – the ones (with Andrew) first called to discipleship (1.16–20) and present with Jesus at the Transfiguration (9.2) – invited by Jesus to go with him and to whom he reveals the torment of his soul, disobey his command to 'watch and pray' and instead fall asleep. They fall asleep three times, just as Jesus goes to pray three times. The contrast between them could not be more emphatic, and it is reinforced soon after by Peter's denial of Jesus three times, as Jesus had predicted (14.30, 66–72).

The irony of the story is biting, and intended as instruction and warning. Those closest to Jesus – in his own day and in ours – are the ones who let him down. Jesus admits his weakness, and through prayer gradually receives strength. The disciples deny their weakness and succumb. Unlike Jesus, they make no progress in faith, because their denial of weakness blocks the way. When the test of their allegiance comes, at the moment of Jesus' arrest, they all run away (14.50–2). Interestingly, in striking contrast to their vocal protestations of loyalty immediately before Gethsemane (14.29–31), throughout the Gethsemane episode itself they say nothing at all. No prayers, no words of encouragement, and only an eloquent silence when Jesus rebukes them for falling asleep: 'they did not know what to answer him' (14.40).

What comes through as a result is Jesus' aloneness and isolation. That itself is part of his struggle with the powers of darkness. It is an aloneness that reaches its dreadful climax on the cross in the cry of God-forsakenness (15.44). Here in Gethsemane, it is prefigured both in the way Jesus separates himself slightly from his disciples (14.33a, 35a) and in the way the disciples remain mute, repeatedly fall asleep and, soon after, run away. It is all Mark's way of saying that this is a cross that Jesus alone has to bear, and that he can do so because he alone is worthy, God's true Son (cf. 1.11; 9.7), the obedient Son of Man (cf. 8.31; 9.31; 10.33–4).

MATTHEW'S VERSION

Matthew's version of the Gethsemane episode is very similar to Mark's. This is probably because not only is it likely that he has used Mark's Gospel as one of his sources, but also because he understands the meaning of Gethsemane in substantially the same ways. Above all, the focus is on Jesus' seeking of God's will in prayer and embracing it as the crisis of his death approaches. For the reader, the story is an encouragement to be like Jesus: to pray to the Father in times of crisis so as not to fall away. But Matthew's version is distinctive at certain points also, and it is important not to blur the differences. The advantage of having more than one version is that we are invited to attend to dimensions of the interpretation of the episode that we might have missed otherwise.

One difference is in the portrayal of Jesus and the disciples. In Mark, the emphasis is on the isolation of Jesus and the incomprehension of the disciples. In Matthew, the emphasis is on Jesus being 'with' his disciples and they being 'with him' (Matthew 26.36a, 38b, 40b). The reason for this is the attention that Matthew draws in his Gospel overall to Jesus as 'God with us' (cf. 1.23; 28.20). According to Matthew, Jesus is God's gracious presence with his people the Church, teaching and guiding the Church through stormy times. Matthew's tendency, therefore, is to emphasize the role of Jesus as a teacher, both by his words and by his example.

That helps to explain why, in Gethsemane, the content of Jesus' prayer is articulated not once (as in Mark) but twice (26.39, 42), thus drawing attention to what Jesus says. It also explains why the content of Jesus' second (and third, noting v. 44b) prayer, slightly different from his first, lines up well with the content of (what we know as) the Lord's Prayer, which Jesus has taught his disciples earlier in the Sermon on the Mount: 'My (Our) Father, ... thy will be done' (26.42; cf. 6.9–10). This is Matthew's way of conveying the insight that Jesus does himself what he teaches others to do. He prays to the Father as he has taught his disciples to pray. He is a good and reliable teacher, for he practises what he preaches. It is as if Matthew is saying to his readers, 'If you want to know what praying the Lord's Prayer is about, follow the example of the Lord himself in the episode in Gethsemane.'

The corollary of this is that the disciples are portrayed as learners in the school of Jesus. Discipleship, for Matthew, is about learning to be like Jesus. That is why they need to be 'with' him and he 'with' them. That is also why Matthew is not as hard on the disciples as Mark. For whereas in Mark the emphasis is on Jesus returning three times to find the disciples sleeping, in Matthew attention focuses more on Jesus as the exemplary person of prayer who goes away three times to pray; and there are no damning words as in Mark's comment that the disciples 'did not know what to answer him' (Mark 14.40b). For if Jesus is a good teacher, then it is important for the disciples in Matthew to be portrayed as (at least moderately) good learners (cf. 13.51–2). It is to the likes of Peter, after all, that a very significant role in founding the Church is given, according to Matthew 16.18–19.

Another difference is in Matthew's exploration of the relationship between Jesus and God. Note that, whereas in Mark Jesus falls on the ground, in Matthew he falls on his face (26.39): a small difference, but it may signify a shift in interpretation from the agony of Jesus to the reverence of Jesus in adopting the traditional posture of obeisance (cf. 2 Samuel 9.6). This is Matthew's way of conveying his understanding of Jesus as God's obedient Son, the one who does his Father's will even in testing times. Consistent with this is the content of Jesus' three prayers; each time Jesus addresses God as '*My* Father' (26.39, 42; cf. v. 44). The emphasis is on Jesus' distinctive, personal relationship with God which his disciples share only in a derivative way. Each time also, Jesus' prayer is that the Father's will be done. Jesus is the unique Son and the obedient Son. As such he serves as *the* authoritative model for his followers.

Such differences do not detract from the impressive correspondence in the interpretations of Gethsemane by Mark and Matthew, but the differences of texture and colouring are important too. We would be deprived of an enormous wealth of insight into the meaning of Gethsemane if we read the Gospels as if they said only the same thing. Thus to risk a generalization: if in Mark the focus is on the costly faithfulness of Jesus and the forbidding loneliness of the way of the cross, in Matthew it is on the exemplary obedience of Jesus as a model for the Church in troubled times.

LUKE'S VERSION

What, then, are we to make of the much shorter account in the Gospel of Luke?[7] In some ways, it is quite different from the versions of Mark and Matthew. It is much shorter. The whole group of disciples remain together: there is no inner circle and Peter is not singled out. Jesus prays only once. His teaching on prayer comes at the beginning and at the end, not in the middle of the story; and the proverb about the willingness of the spirit and the weakness of the flesh is absent. The 'agony' of Jesus follows rather than precedes his prayer (if we take vv. 43–4 as authentic). There is no concluding saying about 'the hour' having come, nor about the imminent betrayal of the Son of Man.

Such differences (and there are more!) are a body-blow to simplistic assertions of the historicity of the event on the basis of appeals to eyewitness testimony. The differences are too great to make a reconstruction possible. But does it matter? It would matter if it was being denied outright that anything of the kind happened, but we do not need to let our reading of the Gospel narratives become captive to extreme and quite unwarranted scepticism of this kind. By the same token, it would matter also if the claim was being made that every detail of the Gospel narratives is 'literally' true. But once again, this is another example of the '100 per cent mentality' that it is wisest to resist if we do not want our reading of the Gospels to become hostages to fortune, captive to the possibility that if one detail becomes dubious, then the whole story becomes worthless or untrue.

As we have seen in our readings of Mark and Matthew, however, there is a better way. Instead of being *distracted* by questions like, 'Did it happen this way or not?', to which it is impossible to give more than a general answer, the very 'differentness' of Luke invites the kind of question, 'Why is the story told this way?' or 'What is the truth of Gethsemane as Luke sees it?' This does justice to the form of the Gospel material as narrative. It also does justice to the natural Christian perception that the truth about Jesus in Gethsemane *can* be told, and *needs* to be told, in more than one way.

Returning to Luke, then, one of the main things to notice is the prominence given to the teaching of Jesus about prayer.[8] The instruction, 'Pray that you may not enter into temptation', frames the whole episode so it must be important (Luke 22.40, 46). From Luke's point of view, this is the 'moral' of the story. It is the commentary on what Jesus himself does, and it is an invitation both to the disciples (*all* of them) and to Luke's readers to do the same, to 'follow' Jesus (cf. v. 39b) in the sense of following his example.

So Jesus is depicted as going to pray in order to prepare himself for the trials ahead. In humility, he moves apart in order to avoid display (cf. 8.9–14); and, reverently, he kneels (22.41). There is no sense either that Jesus prays on impulse (which is more Mark's way of seeing things, perhaps). On the contrary, Luke alone specifically says that Jesus went 'as was his custom' to the Mount of Olives, implying that this is something Jesus does habitually. This should come as no surprise in the context of Luke's narrative as a whole. For, more than any other Gospel writer, Luke emphasizes the importance of prayer in the life of Jesus, especially at moments of decision or revelation or crisis (cf. 3.21–2; 5.16; 6.12; 9.18, 28–9; 10.17–24; 11.1; etc.). Prayer is obviously a crucial element of Jesus' ministry. It is not an optional extra, but what sustains him throughout by keeping him close to God.

The prayer is short, simple and direct – there is no need to badger God – and, like the Lord's Prayer (11.2), begins with the simple word of address, 'Father' (22.42). Then the request to 'remove this cup' is made, for Jesus does not invite suffering. There is no martyr complex here, but the request is made within an overarching commitment to doing the will of God. So it begins, 'if thou art willing', and ends, 'nevertheless, not my will, but thine, be done'.

Although there is considerable debate about the matter, we may assume here that vv. 43–4 are authentic to Luke, rather than being added later. (Even if they were added later, they are certainly not devoid of interest from the point of view of theology and spirituality.) As elsewhere in Luke, Jesus' praying is shown to be effective (cf. 3.21–2; 9.28–9). An angel appears 'to him' – presumably only to him – and strengthens him (22.43). The angel's presence is an indication both of the severity of the struggle – Jesus needs the angel's help – and of the fact that it is a struggle of cosmic, supernatural proportions. In Luke, Satan is never far from the unfolding drama, not least in Luke's narrative of the Passion. In 22.3, Satan enters into Judas Iscariot; in 22.31, Jesus tells Peter that 'Satan demanded to have you'; and at his arrest, Jesus tells his captors, 'this is your hour, and the power of darkness' (22.53b). No wonder, then, given Jesus' awareness of the presence of Satan, that he says to the disciples at the outset, 'Pray that you may not enter into temptation' and that he repeats these words at the end.

The help from the angel – which is the Bible's way of talking about help from God via an intermediary – makes possible an even deeper engagement with God in prayer over the trials to come: 'And being in an agony he prayed more earnestly' (22.44a). Unlike Mark, Jesus is not left on his own. Instead it is perhaps more like what Paul says about the help that the Holy Spirit gives us in our praying: 'for we do not know how to pray as we ought, but the Spirit himself intercedes for us with sighs too deep for words' (Romans 8.26). The graphic description of Jesus' sweat as being 'like great drops of blood falling down upon the ground' shows the intensity of Jesus' praying. He does not stop even to wipe his brow! It may also, with the 'blood' simile, be a premonition of the suffering of the cross that lies ahead.

What about the disciples? In Mark, a corollary of Jesus' isolation and loneliness is the obtuseness and failure of the disciples. In Matthew, a corollary of Jesus' prayer 'master class' is the importance of having the disciples 'with him' to learn. Luke is closer to Matthew than to Mark. For Luke, the corollary of focusing on Jesus' trustful submission and perseverance in prayer is a portrayal of the disciples that is notable for its sympathy. When Jesus comes to the disciples, he finds them sleeping 'for sorrow' (22.45b)! Just as Jesus' own praying is utterly exhausting and needs angelic support to sustain it, so the praying of the disciples is exhausting also and, lacking divine help, they cannot save themselves from succumbing to sleep. However, it is a sleep 'for sorrow', arising out of their identification with Jesus in his tribulation.

Not for nothing has Jesus commended them earlier, at the supper, with the words, 'You are those who have continued with me in my trials' (22.28). Jesus' teaching and his example are so compelling that the disciples' 'following' (22.39) is a natural consequence. Even when Luke comes to narrate the arrest of Jesus, he cannot bring himself to let slip the fact that all the disciples 'forsook him and fled' (Mark 14.50; Matthew 26.56). It is as if Mark seeks to instruct and influence the reader by frequently casting the disciples in a negative light, whereas Luke seeks to instruct and influence by casting them in a positive light. The end result is much the same. But perhaps readers and hearers of the Gospels benefit sometimes from the one, and sometimes from the other: sometimes the 'stick' of Mark, and at other times the 'carrot' of Luke. Any good teacher or preacher might do just the same.

JOHN'S VERSION

The Gospel of John does not have a Gethsemane episode. Instead, there is a long prayer of Jesus in the room where they have eaten (John 17), following which Jesus proceeds with his disciples across the Kidron to 'a garden' where he and his disciples have frequently gathered. Here the arrest takes place straight away (18.1ff.). So, once again, any attempt to determine with any precision 'what actually happened' suffers a serious setback. In a way that for readers only interested in 'the facts' must appear thoroughly perverse, the Gospel of John goes its own way. Like the other Gospels, John's main interests lie elsewhere: not with 'the facts', but with Jesus of Nazareth as the Word of God incarnate, belief in whom brings life out of death. Not that any attempt is made to deceive the reader by falsifying the evidence. Scepticism of this kind is quite unwarranted. Rather, the point is that the reality to which the evidence is made to witness is so transcendent that the entire story has to be told in a different way.

This applies to the Gethsemane tradition in particular. All we have in this Gospel is an echo here and there of what we find more straightforwardly in the Synoptic Gospels. In 18.11, for example, Jesus says to Peter, 'Shall I not drink the cup which the Father has given me?' Here are references to 'the cup' and what 'the Father' has given, but the context is different: not a prayer to God, but a rebuke to Peter, as Jesus hands himself over to his enemies. Jesus has control of events and, in obedience to the Father, goes forward to die.

A louder echo of Gethsemane comes earlier on at a crucial turning-point in John's narrative, in John 12, where Jesus' public ministry to 'the world' reaches its climax, prior to the long private ministry to the disciples, in John 13—17. The climax is the coming of 'some Greeks' to see Jesus. On learning this, Jesus says:

'The hour has come for the Son of man to be glorified. Truly, truly, I say to you, unless a grain of wheat falls into the earth and dies, it remains alone; but if it dies, it bears much fruit. ... Now is my soul troubled. And what shall I say, "Father, save me from this hour"? No, for this purpose I have come to this hour. Father, glorify thy name.' Then a voice came from heaven, 'I have glorified it, and I will glorify it again.' (John 12.23–8)

The echoes of Gethsemane come in the references to 'the hour', the premonition of death, Jesus' soul being 'troubled', the words to God as 'Father', and the request that the Father glorify his name – which is John's way of having Jesus ask for God's will to be done.

Why has John transformed the Gethsemane prayer so radically? And why has he relocated it completely? In relation to the second question, it is worth pointing out that this is not an isolated case. The narrative of the cleansing of the temple, for example, is placed by John not at the end of Jesus' ministry as in the Synoptic Gospels, but at the beginning (2.13–22)! It is as if John is wanting to say that the story of the life of Jesus is a Passion story from beginning to end; that the end of Jesus is there already in the beginning. Of special relevance also is the relocation of the episode of the plotting by the authorities against Jesus to make it become the sequel to the raising of Lazarus (11.45–53), and the relocation of the anointing at Bethany to a point prior to the triumphal entry and once more related to the raising of Lazarus (12.1–8). Chronological precision is clearly not one of John's priorities! What is important to John is how to let the narrative testify to the glory of God revealed in Christ.

It is this motif of 'glory' (Greek: *doxa*) that is the linchpin. The first half of the Gospel narrative concerns the revelation to the world of the glory of God in Jesus the Son of God (cf. 1.14; 2.11). That revelation culminates in the great miracle of the raising of Lazarus from the dead, signifying that Jesus indeed is 'the resurrection and the life'. Typically, the revelation provokes a division. The leaders seek to kill Jesus on grounds of political expediency in order to preserve the temple, the nation and the *status quo* (11.48). Many others, however, acclaim Jesus as king (12.12–19), and some Greeks come to see him (12.20ff.). The reason why the Gethsemane-like tradition is introduced at this point is that it provides John with material from the tradition to express his deeply held conviction that God's glory is revealed supremely in 'the hour' of Jesus' death, a life-giving death anticipated in the death and resurrection of Lazarus and pertaining to people of every kind, including outsiders like 'the Greeks'.

This amazing news is the stuff of revelation. That is why here (and only here) in John's narrative does God speak: 'Then a voice came from heaven, "I have glorified it [my name] and I will glorify it again"' (12.28b). Gethsemane is transformed into a testimony to the glory of God revealed in the Son of God, in the same way that Golgotha is transformed. Just as there is no darkness blotting out the sun in the Johannine Golgotha, so there is no dark wrestling with God in prayer in the Johannine 'Gethsemane'. Indeed, the prayer of Jesus is hardly prayer at all! It has much more the character of proclamation. As Jesus says a little earlier, 'Father, I thank thee that thou hast heard me. I knew that thou hearest me always, but I have said this on account of the people standing by, that they may believe that thou didst send me' (11.41–2; cf. 12.30).

So Jesus' prayer is not really for his own benefit, but for the benefit of those who are listening. It is part of Jesus' witness and proclamation concerning the Father. There is a sense, therefore, in which Jesus does not need to pray. The Gethsemane episode is, from this point of view, redundant. This is so because Jesus' communion with the Father is so close, and his unity with the Father is so complete, that prayer is a reality too deep for words. Jesus does not need to seek the Father's will. His abiding in the Father is so constant that he knows his will already and is obedient to it, even though it will cost him his life (12.23–4, 31–3).

For disciples of Jesus, including readers of John's Gospel, the implication is clear. The complete communion of love between the Father and the Son is to be mirrored in the complete communion of love between disciples and the Father mediated by the Son. This helps to explain why there is no giving of the Lord's Prayer in this Gospel. The challenge instead is to so abide in the love relationship that the Son shares with the Father that the believer's whole life is an act of prayer that hardly needs to be articulated in any set form.[9] That is why Jesus says to the disciples, 'Truly, truly, I say to you, if you ask anything of the Father, he will give it to you in my name' (16.23b). A promise of this kind only makes sense if it is predicated upon a relationship of mutual and wholehearted love and constant communion.

## *Conclusion*

We have been asking the question, 'Why four Gospels?', and have taken as our case-study the Gospel narratives of Jesus in Gethsemane. Doing this has helped us to see a number of things more clearly. First, we would be enormously impoverished in our theology and spirituality if instead of having four Gospels in our canon of Scripture, we had only one. For instead of being invited, in the company of the evangelists, to explore the mystery of Christ's passion as the will of God, we would be tempted to think that the mystery could be grasped in a single account that left no questions unanswered and asked for none. Instead of being invited to explore the many-sidedness of prayer, we would get the impression that prayer means only one thing and is a practice relevant only to occasions of one particular kind.

A related point is that, with four Gospels, we are helped to see that the reality to which the Gospels bear testimony is *too deep to be encapsulated in any one account.* The fourth evangelist makes the same point right at the end of his Gospel when he says, 'But there are also many other things which Jesus did; were every one of them to be written, I suppose that the world itself could not contain the books that would be written' (John 21.25). So we do not need to see a plurality of Gospels in a negative way at all – as if all it does is throw up 'contradictions' that it is our duty to

79

explain in case a single crack in the edifice of Christian truth brings the whole edifice down – the '100 per cent mentality' again! On the contrary, what a plurality of Gospels offers is a repetition that is emphatic and puts a stamp on the way we think about God revealed in Jesus. It offers also a degree of variation that has an *intensifying* effect, inviting us to explore deeper the mystery of God-in-Christ.

Finally, the presence of four Gospels in the canon constitutes a challenge to us as readers. This is not the false challenge to try, by some enormous feat of ingenuity, to flatten out the differences in order to make the Gospels say the same thing or to try to discover 'what actually happened'. Instead it is the challenge to listen with trust to the full range of testimonies to Christ conveyed by the Gospel narratives and, having listened, to allow those testimonies (and others) to leaven our faith and inspire our action in ways that God's Spirit in the Church and in the world shows us to be appropriate.

# 6

# Did It Happen And Does It Matter?

or

## The case of the Fourth Gospel

### *Introduction*

Now we turn to a second case-study to do with what the Gospels are and what they are for. In the last chapter we looked at one particular gospel narrative in all four Gospels. This time we will focus on one Gospel, the Fourth Gospel, taken as a whole. But where is the most appropriate place to begin the interpretation of the Fourth Gospel? We could begin, conventionally, with historical questions about authorship and dating and the circumstances of writing. We can only speculate about these things, however, because the Gospel itself does not provide the answers. In any case, beginning in this way would presuppose that the historian's agenda is the best one, and that once we have found answers to these historical questions, we will then be able to make a satisfactory interpretation of this Gospel.

The historian's agenda, however, does not seem to fit very well with the character of the Gospel itself. Whereas history is interested in Jesus of Nazareth, John's Gospel is interested in Jesus as the Word made flesh (John 1.14–18). History aims to interpret Jesus as a figure of the past, while John's Gospel sets out to confront the reader with Jesus' ever-present claim to divine sonship, in order to provoke a decision for or against him (20.30–1). History is about the accumulation of evidence, whereas John's Gospel is about human testimony to divine revelation, the revelation of God-in-Christ: 'we have beheld his glory, glory as of the only Son from the Father' (1.14). Finally, while history can help us to decide with more or less confidence whether Jesus was this kind of person rather than that, and said and did this rather than the other, the Fourth Gospel offers the reader 'eternal life' through 'receiving' and 'believing in' the Son of Man from heaven (3.16). The Fourth Gospel may certainly be used as a source for historical reconstruction, but that is not necessarily to use it most appropriately.

The interests of the Gospel itself, while they include a concern to pass on traditions about Jesus (since otherwise the evangelist would not have written a *gospel*), lie elsewhere. They lie not with the accumulation of information – for why, then, is the Gospel so selective in what it records? Rather, they focus on providing a basis for *spiritual illumination.* As the Prologue says: 'The true light that enlightens everyone was coming into the world' (1.9 NRSV). Or as Jesus in John says: 'I am the light of the world; whoever follows me will not walk in darkness, but will have the light of life' (8.12 NRSV). Or as the blind man says: 'Whether he is a sinner, I do not know; one thing I know, that though I was blind, now I see' (9.25).

Therefore, perhaps we do more justice to what is actually there by attending to what is involved in reading the Fourth Gospel as *a text of Christian Scripture.* This will have a number of aspects. First, it means that we must give attention to the place of John's Gospel in the canon, as the last in the sequence of the four Gospels, and followed by the Acts of the Apostles, the letters of Paul, the Catholic Epistles, and the Book of Revelation. What is the significance, for the interpretation of John, that it stands where it does in the canon of the New Testament? In terms of most modern New Testament scholarship, this sounds an odd, rather out-of-date, question to ask. But that may be because biblical scholarship has lost sight of the canon as a category of interpretation. For may it not be the case that the placing of this Gospel last in the sequence of the four is a way of saying that, of all the Gospels, John is the one with the clearest insight into the truth about Christ as God incarnate?[1]

Second, it will mean taking seriously what scholars call the kerygmatic quality of the text – referring to the character of the text as a kind of 'preaching' or 'proclamation' (from the Greek, *kerygma*: 'proclamation'). To treat it as historical evidence alone fails to do justice to the Gospel's character as Christian faith-testimony, written to convince and convert and to sustain in faith: ' ... that you may believe that Jesus is the Christ, the Son of God, and that believing you may have life in his name' (20.31). John's Gospel may well be an historical record, but it is not just that. Rather, it is a testimony to the truth about reality as the basis for personal liberation: 'Truly, truly, I say to you, every one who commits sin is a slave to sin. ... So if the Son makes you free, you will be free indeed' (8.34, 36).

There is a personal, existential appeal here, over which historicizing approaches tend to run rough-shod. Such approaches are notorious also in failing to take seriously the place of the Fourth Gospel in the life of the Christian community of faith through the centuries. Not for nothing did Clement of Alexandria describe John as 'the spiritual gospel'; and the Christian doctrines of the Incarnation and the Trinity (to mention the most obvious) would hardly have got off the ground apart from the testimony of the Fourth Gospel.

Finally, reading John as a text of Christian Scripture will involve taking seriously the Gospel as text to be read. The historical paradigm tends to turn the text into a source; and, of course, there is a sense in which that is a legitimate thing to do. The historian addresses the text, interrogates it, and tries thereby to get behind it to some underlying historical event. But if we treat the text as text, then should not our concern be much more to *appreciate* it, rather than interrogate it? And if we treat the text religiously, as a text of Scripture, then ought we not to subordinate our desire to interrogate the text, and instead let the text interrogate us, as Luther and Karl Barth persuasively argued?

This is what believers have always done, traditionally. They have accepted the claim of the text to be religiously authoritative and have sought spiritual illumination from it as Scripture, the Word of God. To put it another way: instead of standing over, or apart from, the text as a source to question and analyse, the believer puts him-/herself *under* the text as divine revelation that leads to God. Instead of breaking the text down in a kind of quasi-scientific analysis, the religious mode of reading is to take the text whole. It is for this reason that a number of interpreters of the Bible are asking whether certain literary approaches to the text, which are more sensitive to the text as text, are not more appropriate than historical approaches.[2]

## The distinctiveness of the Fourth Gospel

One of the main discoveries in the history of the interpretation of John is its distinctiveness.[3] In some circles, there is a tendency to try to explain away this distinctiveness and to 'flatten out' the differences between John and the Synoptics. This is a natural tendency, often the expression of deep religious devotion to Jesus and to God. Nevertheless, it often springs from a very static and monolithic understanding of divine inspiration and of Scripture as the Word of God, an understanding that finds threatening the idea of development and diversity in Scripture and that, ironically, often ends up confusing believing the Bible with believing in God.

It is often the case, also, that resistance to the recognition of the distinctiveness of John arises out of a feeling that to admit the distinctiveness will be to undermine the truth claims of the Jesus of John. It is in the Fourth Gospel, after all, that Jesus so unambiguously identifies himself as the unique Son of God, the only Way to the Father (14.6). To protect this claim, which believers in Jesus so fervently want to affirm, the tendency is to deny the distinctiveness of John (most typically, by harmonizing the Johannine account of Jesus with the accounts of the Synoptics), or to explain the distinctiveness in ways that preserve John's historical credibility.

The harmonizing approach will not work. We need mention just two examples. It is not very likely that Jesus 'cleansed' the temple of Jerusalem twice, once at the beginning of his ministry (so John 2) and once at the end (so the Synoptics). John's placing of the event where he does is much more straightforwardly explained in terms of what he is trying to say as an evangelist than in terms of what might have happened historically. Similarly, it is most unlikely that he was anointed twice in Bethany, once by Mary, the sister of Martha and Lazarus, who anoints Jesus' feet before the triumphal entry into Jerusalem (so John 12.1–8), and a second time by an anonymous woman who anoints Jesus' head after the triumphal entry (so Mark 14.3–9)! Once again, it is what John is trying to say theologically that explains his handling of the tradition rather than what he thought happened historically.

The attempt to safeguard the truth of Jesus' claims according to John by seeking to preserve John's historical credibility is understandable, but misguided. Not that John's Gospel is not historically credible – maybe it is, maybe it isn't. *Sweeping claims one way or the other are not helpful.* It is a mistake, however, to make historical reliability the only touchstone for the truth about Jesus according to John. The criterion of historical reliability is too fragile to bear the weight placed upon it, since it leads to an all-or-nothing kind of position. Doubt on any one point too easily opens up the possibility of doubt wholesale, once we go down this road.

The cracks begin to appear even in what seem to be relatively trivial and straightforward matters. What was the inscription on the titulus on Jesus' cross, for example? Mark has, 'The King of the Jews' (15.26); Matthew has, 'This is Jesus the King of the Jews' (27.37); Luke has, 'This is the King of the Jews' (23.38); and John has, 'Jesus of Nazareth, the King of the Jews' (19.19), and also goes on to tell us that the inscription was written in Hebrew, Latin and Greek (19.20). It is surprising, given all the eyewitnesses to the crucifixion, that there is such variety. (The apocryphal Gospel of Peter, 11, has yet another version: 'This is the King of Israel'!) Ingenious attempts to harmonize the versions are possible, but they soon begin to look like attempts to paper over the historical cracks.

A more serious example for defenders of Johannine historicity (as well as for defenders of the historicity of all four Gospels) is the question, 'What were Jesus' last words from the cross?' In

Mark and Matthew, it is the cry of desolation (Mark 15.34 par.); in Luke, Jesus prays, 'Father, into thy hands I commit my spirit!' (23.46); and in John, Jesus proclaims, 'It is finished!' (19.30). The differences are undeniable. But what a shame it would be for the *religious appreciation* of these various 'last words', in their respective contexts, if their meaning and significance for faith were made captive to questions of historical authenticity.

This brings us to a second reason for not making historical reliability the touchstone for the truth of the Johannine witness to Jesus. It is that faith and personal commitment become bound by the canons of historical rationality. If historical reason is given such a pivotal role, then the faith of the believer stands at the mercy of the historian. The irony of the conservative's appeal to historicity as the main bulwark of faith, is that faith becomes highly vulnerable to the findings of the *secular* enterprise of history. Either that, or it makes its appeal to 'bad' history – that is, to history that is not intellectually respectable.

This is not to advocate a divorce between faith and historical investigation, just as we would not advocate a divorce between faith and theology. For both history and theology are legitimate and necessary enterprises of inquiry that provide believers with guidance about what makes sense in the life of faith from the point of view of contemporary rationality.[4] It is a serious mistake, however, to try to prove the truth of faith claims on the basis of history alone. For, all of a sudden, faith can easily become a form of *rationalism*, very much in the spirit of the age in which we live. Instead of trying to live by faith in response to the love of God revealed in Christ, Christianity becomes a matter of trying to prove whether or not Jesus did claim, as a matter of fact, to be the Son of God, as the Fourth Gospel says.

In what follows, therefore, what we need to do is, first, see how distinctive the Fourth Gospel is in relation to the other three Gospels; second, suggest some reasons why it is distinctive; and, by way of a conclusion, draw attention to the wider implications of the interpretation of John in its canonical context.

## *John and the Synoptics: what they have in common*

In comparing John and the Synoptics, it is important to recognize what they have in common. One of the reasons for the tendency to harmonize the Gospel accounts is the fact that, in general terms, the story they tell is the same. Thus, all four Gospels depict a Jesus who is a miracle worker and a teacher, who is crucified and raised from the dead. Unlike Paul's letters, for instance, all the Gospels reflect a concern to pass on an account of the life of Jesus, as well as having an interest in his death. Similarly, all four Gospels share a concern to preserve traditions of the past of Jesus, as well as to experience Jesus spiritually in the present.

In addition, John and the Synoptics have episodes of Jesus' life in common. There is an initial encounter with John the Baptist, even though, in the Fourth Gospel, he is never called 'the Baptist'. There are stories of the call of disciples, too, even though John gives prominence to disciples (such as Andrew, Philip and Nathanael) who are mentioned only in passing in the Synoptics. There is the story of Jesus' public ministry, which begins in Galilee, leads to opposition, and culminates in arrest, trial and crucifixion in Jerusalem, with resurrection appearances in both Galilee (as in Mark and Matthew) and Jerusalem (as in Luke). In terms of specific incidents, one thinks also of the cleansing of the temple, the healing of the official's son, the miraculous feeding by the Sea of Galilee, the walking on the sea, the healing of a blind man, the anointing of Jesus before his death by a woman, the triumphal entry, the betrayal by Judas, the denial by Peter, the Last Supper, the trial before Pilate, the crucifixion, and the discovery of the empty tomb.

Then there is sayings material where the Johannine tradition overlaps with Synoptic tradition. Thus, the 'bread of life' discourse in John 6, where Jesus says, 'the bread [*artos*] which I shall give for the life of the world is my flesh' (6.51), compares with the saying of Jesus at the Last Supper, in Mark 14.22, 'This [bread: *artos*] is my body'. The language Jesus uses of himself in the footwashing (John 13.12ff.) is reminiscent of Luke 22.27: 'I

87

am among you as one who serves [*ho diakonōn*]'. The teaching of the love commandment, in John 13.34, 14.15, etc., overlaps with Jesus' teaching about love of neighbour, in Mark 12.31 and parallels. The expectation of hatred from the world (John 15.18–21) can be compared with the final beatitude (Matthew 5.11f. par.). The sending of the disciples by Jesus into the world (John 13.16, 20; 15.20; 17.3, 8; etc.) compares with the Synoptic commissionings (Matthew 10.24; Luke 6.40). Being 'born again/from above' in order to see the kingdom of God (John 3.3) reminds us of the Synoptic traditions about the necessity of becoming 'like a child' in order to enter the kingdom of God (Matthew 18.3; Mark 10.15 par. Luke 18.17). As a final example, the presentation of Jesus as the Good Shepherd who lays down his life for the sheep (John 10) reminds us of the Lucan version of the parable of the lost sheep, in Luke 15.4–7.

A fourth aspect of broad agreement between John and the Synoptics, even if only at the most general level, is narrative structure. We can identify an opening section, which has a prologue, Jesus' baptism, and the call of disciples in Galilee; a central section, with a miraculous feeding, a walking on water, and the Johannine version of Peter's christological confession (6.68f.), all in Galilee; and a final section, with the entry into Jerusalem, the Last Supper, final words to the disciples, Jesus' arrest, trial, crucifixion and burial, the discovery of the empty tomb, and appearances of the risen Lord.

D. Moody Smith's comment on the overall picture of what John and the Synoptics have in common is worth quoting:

> Common elements can be adduced in such numbers it is not surprising that throughout most of Christian history efforts have been made to synchronize or otherwise harmonize John with the other canonical Gospels. As far as we know, this effort began in earnest with Tatian's Diatessaron, a late second-century composite drawn from the canonical Gospels, and perhaps from other sources. It continues down to the present in imaginative, non-scientific books and films, not to mention sermons,

about Jesus. Yet the task of combining John with the synoptics is not an easy one, and the attempts to do so have never been entirely plausible or convincing, despite the best efforts of ancient and subsequent authors. The reasons for this have to do with the differing character of the Johannine and synoptic accounts and of the material of which they are composed.

(D. Moody Smith, *John* (Philadelphia, Fortress Press, 1976), p. 3.)

## John and the Synoptics: where they differ

As is widely recognized now, John and the Synoptics differ at many points, so we can only touch on the most significant ones here. However, these will begin to show something of the extent of the 'Johannine problem'.

First, they differ in their accounts of the origins of Jesus. Mark begins his story of Jesus with the appearance of John the Baptist at the River Jordan. Matthew and Luke take us a stage further back, and provide us with genealogies, birth and (in the case of Luke) infancy narratives. The Fourth Gospel shows no interest in the birth and boyhood of Jesus, and is not concerned (unlike Matthew and Luke) with proving that Jesus was Messiah because he was born in Bethlehem, the city of David (cf. 7.40ff.). Instead, John focuses all our attention on his identification of Jesus as the incarnation of the pre-existent Logos of God: 'And the Word became flesh and dwelt among us, full of grace and truth. ... For the law was given through Moses; grace and truth came through Jesus Christ' (1.14, 17).

There are also major differences in the accounts of Jesus' miracles. Whereas in the Synoptics the demon exorcisms bulk large – in Mark, for instance, Jesus' first miracle is an exorcism, which becomes the basis for instant fame throughout Galilee (Mark 1.21–8) – in John there are none at all. Why is this so? Was John embarrassed about portraying Jesus as a man of his time? Or did John only want to concentrate on the more spectacular miracles in order, perhaps, to distinguish Jesus from the relatively common exorcistic practice and practitioners of his day? Or were there theological reasons for his neglect of the exorcism traditions – to do, perhaps, with John's understanding of the kingdom of God and the defeat of Satan, aspects of what we might call, using doctrinal language, Johannine eschatology?

As well as no exorcisms, there is no account of the Transfiguration in John; this event, which is so pivotal in Mark, is missing completely. This is especially surprising in view of the evangelist's strong interest in demonstrating the divine 'glory' (*doxa*) of Jesus. Turning to miracles of healing, we note that John has no precise parallel to any of the Markan healings, although there are several Johannine stories of a similar sort (e.g. the healing of the blind man in chapter 9). Also, John reduces the number of Jesus' miracles of healing to just four, which is a fraction of the number in the Synoptic tradition.

The interpretation of the miracles is another point of contrast. In the Synoptics, the miracles are pointers to the coming of the kingdom of God: 'But if it is by the finger of God that I cast out demons, then the kingdom of God has come upon you' (Luke 11.20 par.). In John, the miracles are 'signs' (*sēmeia*), whose purpose is to reveal the identity of Jesus as the divine Son. So, at the end of the first miracle story, the narrator comments: 'This, the first of his signs, Jesus did at Cana in Galilee, and manifested his glory; and his disciples believed in him' (2.11). These sign-miracles become occasions for extended revelatory discourses which are quite unique to John; and the focus is always on Jesus' own identity – as the bread of life (chapter 6), the light of the world (chapter 9), the resurrection and the life (chapter 11), and so on. Jesus the proclaimer of the kingdom, in the Synoptics, becomes Jesus the King, in John; and the miracles are the signs of his kingship (cf. 6.15).

John's account of the ministry of Jesus is distinctive too. Here we note that even though it starts in Galilee, in the north, its main location is in Judea, in the south. Why this neglect of Jesus the Galilean? In Mark, by contrast, Galilee is the setting for the whole first half of the narrative, and Jesus is only in Jerusalem for the last week of his life. Also, whereas the Synoptics have

Jesus go to Jerusalem only once, at the end of his ministry and as the climax of his prophetic mission, John has Jesus visit Jerusalem three times, each time on the occasion of a major festival. One of the effects of this, by the way, is to present Jesus' ministry in the predominantly urban setting (of Jerusalem), rather than the more rural one of the Synoptics.

Noticeable too is the way that the Jesus of John stands over against and apart from Judaism and the Jews in a way hardly paralleled in the Synoptics. In 8.17, for example, Jesus refers to the Torah as 'your law'; and in 8.56 he speaks of 'your father Abraham'. In return, Jesus is suspected of being a Samaritan (8.48); and, at a slightly earlier point in the narrative, the Jews seriously wonder if Jesus is intending to go to the Diaspora to teach the Greeks (7.35). There is a strong sense – stronger in John than in the Synoptics – that Jesus no longer belongs in Judaism, but instead somewhere else. This is all of a piece with the general point that the language used by the Jesus of John is markedly more 'Christian' than is the case with the Jesus of the Synoptics.

When we turn next to a comparison of the teaching of Jesus in John and in the Synoptics we find, perhaps more than anywhere else, that the distinctiveness of the Johannine Jesus comes to the fore. Thus, if we attend to the style and form of the teaching, we note that there are none of the pronouncement stories so common in the Synoptics – that is, short episodes where a question is posed of Jesus and the episode climaxes with an authoritative, epigrammatic saying (e.g. Mark 2.23–8, the controversy story over the plucking of grain on the sabbath, which ends, 'And he said to them, "The sabbath was made for man, not man for the sabbath; so the Son of man is lord even of the sabbath"'; cf. 12.13–17).

In John, there are no sharp, pithy sayings so well known from the Synoptics, such as 'Foxes have holes, and the birds of the air have nests; but the Son of man has nowhere to lay his head'; or, 'No one who puts his hand to the plough and looks back is fit for the kingdom of God' (Luke 9.58, 62). The Jesus of John speaks in figures and allegories (e.g. John 10.1ff.; 15.1ff.), but he does not teach in parables in the way that is so characteristic of the Jesus of the Synoptics. In particular, there are no parables of the kingdom, such as those collected together in Mark 4 and Matthew 13. Instead, there are long, convoluted discourses, in which a theme is taken and developed at length, in a rather homiletic style and with a strongly Christian flavour. The discourse on Jesus as the bread from heaven (John 6.25–59), with its strong eucharistic overtones, is a classic instance of this.

In addition, the content of the teaching is distinctive. In general, it is true to say that most of the Synoptic teaching is not in John, and most of the Johannine teaching is not in the Synoptics! Whereas the Synoptic Jesus proclaims the coming of the kingdom of God, Jesus in John is never shown as publicly proclaiming the kingdom. Only five times in John does he speak of the kingdom; and these occurrences come in just two private conversations, with Nicodemus (3.3, 5) and with Pilate (18.36) – and in the latter case, Jesus speaks of '*my* kingdom' rather than 'the kingdom of God'. In the Synoptics, by contrast, 'kingdom' is used forty-seven times in Matthew, eighteen times in Mark, and thirty-seven times in Luke. Putting this difference in broad doctrinal terms, the shift is from eschatology in the Synoptics to christology in John. Or, perhaps a little more precisely, the shift is from future eschatology in the Synoptics to an eschatology almost completely swallowed up by christology in John. Consistent with this is the fact that there are no apocalyptic Son of Man sayings in John, of the kind found, for example, in Mark 14.61f.

Striking also is the fact that there is no teaching in public about morality, questions relating to customary observances and issues to do with the conduct of everyday life (like divorce and re-marriage, the payment of taxes, obedience to the civil authorities, and the like). Another way of putting this is to observe that John does not have a version of the Sermon on the Mount. Instead, all we find is teaching of a very general kind in private to the disciples: the teaching of the 'new commandment' about brotherly love (e.g. 15.12ff.). Characteristic of this kind of difference is the contrast between Jesus' teaching in Matthew 5.14ff.,

'You are the light of the world. ... Let your light so shine before men, that they may see your good works and give glory to your Father who is in heaven', and Jesus' teaching in John 8.12, 'I am the light of the world; he who follows me will not walk in darkness, but will have the light of life.' This latter saying, in John, is one of a number of 'I AM' sayings which are also quite distinctive to the Johannine Jesus, and mark again the decisive shift towards a concentration on christology in the Fourth Gospel.

## Explaining the distinctiveness of the Johannine Jesus

There can be no question of denying the distinctiveness of the Johannine Jesus in comparison with the Jesus of the Synoptics. Nor can there be any question of resorting to attempts to harmonize the four Gospels: the differences are too great. So what are the possible ways forward in dealing with this 'problem'?

One approach is to argue that the Synoptics give us history and the Fourth Gospel gives us theology – tells us what the history 'really means'. There is something in this: it is a kind of intuitive response to a number of things. First, it is a response to the apparent fact that the Fourth Gospel goes into things much more deeply than the Synoptics, by being more selective in what it records, and by exploring more fully and with greater intensity the spiritual and christological dimensions of sayings and events – as, for instance, when the feeding miracle becomes an opportunity to expound on Jesus as the ultimate spiritual nourishment. Second, it is a response, perhaps, to the fact that the Fourth Gospel is the *fourth* of the Gospels, and might be expected, from a canonical perspective, to give us the definitive position on Jesus and his significance for faith.

But this view is inadequate in at least two respects. It does not do justice to the theological and kerygmatic character of the Synoptics – that is, to the fact that they are not 'straight history' either – something that various types of Gospel criticism have made abundantly clear in the critical study of the last century or more. It does not do justice, either, to the historical character of the Fourth Gospel. For there can be little doubt that John thought that he was writing history, even if history of a special sort – since, after all, its subject was very special.

A second approach is to argue that, just as the Synoptics are historical, so too is John; that the Jesus of John is the Jesus of the Synoptics, but that John gives us a different side to Jesus and incorporates new information about him. One form of this argument is to say that John gives us what Jesus taught in private rather than in public, and/or that he gives us what Jesus taught in the south, in his controversies with the authorities in Jerusalem, rather than what Jesus taught in Galilee. Whatever one thinks of this latter hypothesis, there is good reason for regarding John as having serious historical interests.

After all, John writes a Gospel, not a theological treatise – even though he does not call his writing a 'gospel', as Mark does (Mark 1.1). Also, John is at pains to stress the prominent role of witnesses, at various points (especially 1.14; 19.35; 21.24f.; cf. 1 John 1.1ff.). Yet again, others have drawn attention to various pieces of topographical information scattered throughout the narrative, which show, it can be fairly claimed, a concern on the writer's part to get the details right: Aenon near Salim (3.23), the pool of Siloam (9.7), the pool of Bethzatha/Bethesda in Jerusalem with the five porticoes (5.2), are three of thirteen cases in point. Finally, we may mention thorough investigations of the Johannine tradition such as that of C. H. Dodd.[5] Dodd showed that it is very likely that early tradition lies behind the Fourth Gospel, tradition independent of that developed in the Synoptic Gospels and at least as reliable in certain areas – the tradition of the Passion being a case in point.

Nevertheless, as with the claim that John is primarily theological, the claim that John is primarily historical faces difficulties as well. First, there is the apparently insuperable difficulty of the differences of content between John and the Synoptics. For example, if the 'I AM' sayings were part of the original Jesus tradition, it is inconceivable that only John should incorporate them and that the Synoptic evangelists should neglect them entirely. If the footwashing and the farewell discourses of John 13—17 were part of the original Jesus tradition, it is, again, extremely difficult to explain the accounts of the Last Supper in the Synoptics, just as it is difficult to explain the absence of the 'words of institution' in John – and so on.

A second difficulty concerns the style of John's account. The suggestion that John's account is different because he supplies the private instruction or the teaching of Jesus in Jerusalem, and that in these different settings Jesus adopted different styles, which John's Gospel reflects, fails completely to reckon with the fact that the language of John is consistent throughout, that it is consistently Johannine, that it is very much of a piece with the First Epistle of John, and that it is consistently different from the Synoptics. If any further confirmation were wanted, we could note in addition that the teaching of John the Baptist in the Fourth Gospel shows the same characteristics: it is consistently Johannine and consistently different from the John the Baptist of the Synoptics.

For various good reasons, therefore, it will not do to try to account for the distinctiveness of John by arguing that the Fourth Gospel is either wholly theological (whereas the Synoptics are historical), or wholly historical (but in a way different from the Synoptics). More plausible, is the view that John's Gospel, *like* the Synoptics, is a theological interpretation of history. As James Dunn puts it:

> John's Gospel is an account of Jesus refracted through the prism of John's theology and literary style. And the discourses in particular are best seen as meditations or sermons intended to draw out the significance of what Jesus said and did. ... The Synoptic Gospels, if you like, are more like a portrait of Jesus; John's Gospel is more like an impressionist painting of Jesus. Both present the real Jesus, but in very different ways.
>
> (James D. G. Dunn, *The Evidence for Jesus* (London, SCM, 1985), p. 43.)

Precisely what factors were influential in encouraging the kind of 'impressionist painting' he actually paints is a very important area of historical and literary investigation – things to do with the nature of John's sources, the historical situation of the Johannine community, the identity of the evangelist, influences from the religious thought-world of the time, and so on. This is an exciting area of investigation which continues to attract the interest of readers of John around the world.

## Conclusion: some implications

In conclusion, it is worth reflecting a little further on the implications for Christian theology and spirituality of the 'discovery' of the distinctiveness of John.

The first point to make is that the distinctiveness of the Fourth Gospel is sheer gain *for theology*. For this Gospel shows that, at a very early stage in Christian history, it came to be felt that the only adequate way of responding to Jesus and the salvation he brought to men and women was to accord him divinity and to present him as the Word of God incarnate. As such, John represents a major challenge to the tendency in some scholarly circles to distinguish sharply between the Jesus of history and the Christ of faith, often on the undeclared assumption that the real Jesus is the former, the property of historical investigation, and that the Christ of faith is 'mere myth' or merely the preserve of those with religious interests. For John, however, the Jesus of history and the Christ of faith are one and the same; and the challenge to the reader of this Gospel, in every epoch, is to see whether or not this is so.

The second point is that the distinctiveness of the Fourth Gospel is a gain also *for ecclesiology*, i.e. for what it means to be the Church. By being different, it gives access to faith to readers who might otherwise be untouched on the basis of a reading of the Synoptics or Paul or the Epistle to the Hebrews or the Apocalypse. It contributes, in other words, to the catholicity of the Church, to the vocation of the Church to be inclusive because the grace of God on which it is founded is inclusive. Nicholas Lash says: '"Catholic" is what the church is under obligation to seek to become, and the quest for catholicity is frustrated by the exclusion from its symbol-stock, whether by accident or design, of any of the irreducibly diverse languages that constitute the memory and interpret the experience of mankind.'6 John's Gospel is one such 'symbol-stock', and its contribution to the diversity of the Christian canon of Scripture is a contribution to the Church's vocation to catholicity.

Third, and finally, the discovery of the distinctiveness of John is a gain *for Christian spirituality*. In particular, the 'refusal' of John to be harmonizable with the Synoptics means that one-sided claims to know 'the' truth about Jesus are without justification. Such claims are able to be seen for what they sometimes are: strategies of fear masquerading in the guise of religious faith. According to John, however, 'the truth will make you free'. Part of John's contribution to that liberating process is its offer of a vision of Christ and of the gospel that differs in important respects from that of other New Testament writings.

# 7

## What About 'Problem Texts'?

### or

### Is the Bible good news
### for women?

### *Introduction*

We have had occasion several times already to observe that, for various reasons, the Bible is 'a difficult book' which needs to be interpreted with care and skill if it is to be a source of life for those who read it. This brings us to the question, 'What about "problem texts"?' Examples are not difficult to think of. In the Old Testament, there is the story of the sacrifice of Isaac in Genesis 22, which could appear to modern eyes as a clear case of child abuse. Then there are the accounts of Israelite 'holy war', where God commands that all the inhabitants of the enemy cities – men, women, children, and even household animals – are to be put to the sword and no prisoners taken (cf. Numbers 31). What, we might ask, could be 'holy' about that?

In the New Testament, the examples are not quite as dramatic perhaps, but the problematic nature of many texts is real none the less. In recent years, the portrayal of the Jews in the Gospels (John in particular) has been seen by some as anti-semitic. Others have long regarded the Gospel teaching about the 'eternal fire' of divine wrath (cf. Matthew 25.41,46) or Paul's doctrine of predestination in Romans 9—11 as immoral. Yet others have come to regard the New Testament teaching about the place of women in Church and society as fundamentally sexist (cf. 1 Corinthians 11.2–16; 14.34–6; 1 Timothy 2.8–15). It is this latter example that we will focus on in this chapter as a way into the larger question of what to do about 'problem texts'.

## Is the Bible 'good news' for women?

There can be little doubt that there is more disagreement than ever before over the question, 'Is the Bible good news for women?' As in so many areas, the consensus has broken down and is fiercely contested. For many, the Bible remains the touchstone for how women and men are to live and how life in family, Church and society is to be conducted.[1] For many others, the Bible has little or no authority because it belongs so obviously to a bygone age and its teaching is neither credible nor helpful.[2] Others, yet again, find themselves somewhere in the middle, caught between feelings of loyalty to the Bible and a bewildering sense that modern people do not, and cannot, take the Bible seriously any more.[3]

The way in which the Bible can become a 'problem text' for women – and, of course, not just women – is illustrated powerfully by the following item from the *Independent* newspaper, Friday, 12 September 1988:

A Dublin woman wants the Bible banned because she claims that it endorses the sexual abuse of young girls, glorifies violence and supports mutilation.

Anne Spicer has made a formal written request to the republic's Censorship of Publications Board, which has banned a small library of internationally popular books over the years.

She said: 'Mutilation and genocide, coupled with graphic obscenity and ritual murder, is a prominent theme, and, indeed many of the heroes and heroines are extolled for their murderous ability and promiscuous prowess. ...'

Mrs Spicer, 34, a mother of three, asked the board to explain a system that allowed the banning of publications such as Dr Alex Comfort's *The Joy of Sex*, which 'seeks to enhance or portray sexual techniques,' while allowing the Bible and 'its obscene incitement to crime' to remain on sale.

'Why should *The Joy of Sex* be banned? Are people not supposed to enjoy sex? If there is going to be censorship, then violence should be on the menu – the Bible is riddled with it.'

Mrs Spicer singled out sections of the scriptures. She claimed that Deuteronomy 22 endorsed the murder of brides who were not virgins and quoted the passage which reads: '... but if a thing is true, that the tokens of virginity were not found in the young woman, then they shall bring the young woman to the door of her father's house, and the men of the city shall stone her to death ... so you shall purge the evil from your midst.'

She also quoted a passage from Deuteronomy 25 to support her charge that mutilation is advocated by the Bible: 'If a woman puts out her hand and seizes him by the private parts, then you shall cut off her hand, your eyes shall have no pity.' Mrs Spicer said that sexual abuse and slavery occurred in passages where Moses told the Israelites not to kill captured young virgins but to keep them for their own use.

The board said that the submission would be considered.

(Quoted, with gratitude, by permission of the publishers of the *Independent* newspaper.)

One of the issues that lie behind these kinds of complaints and objections is that of interpretation: 'What does the Bible mean for Christians today?' The aim of this chapter is to discuss issues of method in interpretation with a view to suggesting that the original question is wrongly put. Instead of asking, 'Is the Bible good news for women?', the question we should be asking is much more of the kind, 'What sort of people do we need to become so that we are able to read the Bible in ways that are life-giving [for women or whoever]?' In other words, more consideration should be given to the possibility that it is not the Bible that should be the main bone of contention. Rather, the focus ought to be more on what is going on *on this side* of the

100

text: who it is who is reading the Bible and what it might mean to read the Bible well and wisely.

## The right place to start

Knowing the right place to start is a critical issue, often over-looked. One very common approach is to start with the Bible. Interestingly, this tends to be the approach of both conservative fundamentalists and liberal historical critics. Both groups, faced with the question 'Is the Bible good news for women?' assume that the obvious and correct thing to do is to go 'back to the Bible', find the texts about women, and see what they have to say. Many reports issued by church bodies and ecclesiastical authorities likewise begin with opening chapters on 'what the Bible teaches', the obvious intention being to lay the firm foundations for what follows on interpretation and application. The implicit assumption here is that interpretation and application *follow* the laying of 'objective' biblical foundations. In fact, of course, going 'back to the Bible' is a much more complex process than this, involving the subjectivity of the reader(s) as well as the givenness of the text. For it is just as much the case that interpretation and application *precede and shape* our reading of the Bible as the other way round.[4]

Nevertheless, in some ways, paying due attention to 'what the Bible teaches' is a common sense and unobjectionable way of proceeding. Obviously, an important ingredient of any attempt to answer contemporary questions will be to try to find the relevant biblical material and see what it says. We cannot do without what has come to be called 'the horizon of the text', and it is the goal of exegesis and historical criticism to help us clarify that horizon. But there are problems lying not too far beneath the surface of this apparently common-sense, 'objective' approach.

First, there is the problem of what model of the Bible and Bible reading is being presupposed. To put it in the form of a question, What is involved in using the Bible as *a source* of information or instruction? Is the Bible understood best along archaeological lines, as something to go back to or dig into? Operating on the assumption that this is so, the conservative fundamentalist quarries the Bible for the appropriate proof-texts, ascertains the 'plain sense' of the text, and seeks then to apply it in (what is believed to be) a straightforward, rational way to everyday life. Operating (ironically) on basically the same assumption, the liberal historical critic also quarries the Bible, ascertains the plain sense of the text, and then, if he or she is religiously disposed, tries to weigh up rationally whether it is applicable or not, taking its historically conditioned character into account.

But what if the Bible is something more than a source to be quarried and analysed in the privacy either of the believer's 'quiet time' or of the critic's study? What if interpreting the Bible is not best understood as a kind of 'archaeological dig' for hidden treasure or historical facts? What if the Bible is more like the text of a Shakespearean play or the score of a Beethoven symphony, where true interpretation involves a group of people doing a performance, and where the meaning of the text or score will vary somewhat from one performance to another depending on who is performing and what the circumstances are? As we shall see in the next chapter, a number of writers have begun to explore this alternative model of interpreting the Bible.[5] Its advantage is that it brings the reading of the Bible back into the process of Christian community-formation and celebration and places responsibility on that community to read the text in ways that build up rather than destroy.

Related to the first problem is the problem of the 'Little Jack (or Jill!) Horner' approach to the Bible. How adequate are approaches to the Bible that select out the 'purple passages' about women, or isolate the stories about women, or focus in a proof-texting way on those texts that support a particular position, whether for or against women? This approach is very common – perhaps *the* most common. Think, for example, of the enormous attention devoted to New Testament texts like Galatians 3.28 ('... there is neither male nor female ... in Christ Jesus'), or 1 Corinthians 11.2–16 ('... the head of a woman is her husband ...'), or 1 Timothy 2.8–15 ('Let a woman learn in silence with all submissiveness ...'). Even on single verses, like the one about 'headship' in 1 Corinthians 11.3, the exegetical literature can be enormous.[6] But, for all the exegetical effort, agreement is hard to reach, often because the text itself is opaque to readers in the late twentieth century (as it may have been also to readers in the first!).

There are certain dangers in this proof-text kind of approach. For instance, there is the danger of trivializing Scripture, as if all that matters is whether or not selected texts (can be made to) speak for or against women. This is not to deny the general point that 'women's issues' are important. What is questionable, however, is the wisdom of so focusing women's issues on a certain kind of Bible reading that such issues become the dominant – sometimes almost exclusive – agenda, and the Bible becomes little more than a battleground of competing special interest groups. Instead of being 'a lamp unto our feet and a light unto our path', Scripture is trivialized by being taken hostage by interest groups, and at the same time the issue of women is trivialized as well. To put the point another way, the Bible was *not* written 'in memory of her' (the title of Elisabeth Schüssler Fiorenza's ground-breaking feminist study of 1983): even though it is quite legitimate for writers like Fiorenza to engage in the historical task of making early Christian women visible. Rather, a Christian theological view of the Bible has to affirm that the Bible is much more 'the book of *God*', partly recognizable as such not least because of what it says about women.

Then there is the danger that the Bible will not be allowed to speak as *one book*, but instead becomes fractured and fragmented into many isolated, or even opposing, parts. So, for example, the account of the creation of the man and the woman in Genesis 1 is played off against the account in Genesis 2—3; Jesus' attitude to women is played off against the Gospel writers' or Paul's; Paul the liberationist is played off against the patriarchalism of the Pastoral Epistles, and so on.[7] Now this is not to deny that there are often very significant differences between one part of the

Bible and another, not least on 'the question of women'; and it is important not to encourage a simplistic harmonizing of one Bible passage with another.

What it is necessary to point out, however, is the destructive potential of these kinds of interpretative strategy; for, in the end, the Bible can be dispensed with altogether. Those who 'flatten out' the text of the Bible by a process of harmonization so that it is always saying the same thing, undermine the Bible by making it monolithic, static and ultimately uninteresting, since once you have decided what the Bible says you don't really need it any more. Those, on the other hand, who divide up the Bible by setting one text over against another also undermine it, this time by divesting it of coherence and weakening its authority. What is needed instead is a way of reading the Bible that transcends these alternatives and allows the Bible to function as life-giving, revelatory Scripture for the Church.

Also, there is the danger that the text becomes captive to tribal interests of one kind or another, whether conservative fundamentalism, liberal biblical criticism, feminism (of various possible kinds), and so on. When this happens, the meaning of the text (and even more the truth of the text) tends to get confused with the political-cum-pragmatic question of whether or not the text can be *used* to support the identity and self-understanding of the group concerned. The corollary of all this is a tendency towards scapegoating. For example, the Bible becomes the scapegoat for the anxieties of feminists (the 'blame it all on the Bible' approach), or feminists and women in general become the scapegoat for the anxieties of the loyalists (the 'blame it all on the feminists' approach), or the historical critics adopt an approach along the lines of 'a plague on both your houses' and withdraw to issues of an apparently more 'neutral' kind.

Then there is the issue, 'What constitutes an appropriate set of *expectations* to bring to the biblical text?' For some, it is essential to approach the text in a spirit of trust, itself based upon a 'high' view of the Bible as the Word of God. For others, it is necessary to approach the text from a stance of systematic suspicion, on the assumption that the Bible is either outdated (so the modernist) or a weapon of oppression (so the feminist). But it is rarely acknowledged that both the loyalist position and the revisionist (or rejectionist) positions are two sides of the same coin, according to which the main issue is whether or not the Bible can be trusted. The Enlightenment tendency to put God in the dock for cross-examination is transferred here to the Bible. Now it is the Bible that is placed in the dock, with some quoting proof-texts in its defence, and others quoting proof-texts on behalf of the prosecution. Instead of allowing ourselves to be judged by Scripture as 'the book of God', we become its judges. Instead of learning in the Christian community the kinds of skill and wisdom necessary to faithful interpretation and enactment, we 'objectify' the text either as a book to be obeyed or as a book to be dismissed.

Yet another problem is that of assuming that the text has only *one meaning*, the literal meaning, and that this is to be ascertained rationally using common sense in one form or another – that is, the common sense of 'the man [*sic*] on the Clapham omnibus' or the common sense arising out of the application of historical criticism. On this view, once *the* meaning of the text has been established, it is a matter simply of 'applying' it to the modern world, or of disregarding it as irrelevant to the modern world. But why assume that the meaning of the biblical text is univocal? It is one thing to resist the idea that 'anything goes' and that there are no limits to what a text may mean; it is another to go to the opposite extreme of saying that the text has one true meaning only (which usually happens to be the meaning *my group* holds to).

However, there is a more moderate position in between the extremes, with strong precedent in the Bible itself as well as in the exegesis of the early Church and the Middle Ages.[8] According to this view, a text may have meanings over and above that intended by the original author, meanings that the author was unable to see or that the author did not anticipate. This opens up the possibility that texts that appear to subordinate or neglect women may be read now in ways that are affirming of women,[9] and, conversely, that texts that appear to affirm women may be read now in ways that oppress them.

It is *the character of the reading community* that will determine in large measure in which direction the process of interpretation goes. This has been well argued recently by Stephen E. Fowl and L. Gregory Jones, who put the point this way:

> Thus Christian communities are central for the ongoing task of enabling people to become wise readers of Scripture. To become wise readers of Scripture, we need to acquire a range of skills and virtues manifested in Christian discipleship. These skills and virtues are given their shape and form under the guidance of the Holy Spirit in and through the particular friendships and practices of Christian communities. They both are the prerequisite for, and the result of, wise readings of Scripture. These skills and virtues not only enable wise reading but also faithful practice. They show forth a witness to God's ways with the world. ... Christian communities must be aware of the possibilities of inter-preting Scripture in such a way that it supports rather than subverts corrupt and sinful practices. This means that we Christians will need to learn to read the Scriptures 'over-against ourselves' rather than simply 'for ourselves'. This is the sense in which our 'readings of the texts' involve allowing the texts to provide readings of us.
>
> (Stephen E. Fowl and L. Gregory Jones, *Reading in Communion. Scripture and Ethics in Christian Life* (London, SPCK, 1991), pp. 35–6, 41–2.)

Finally, there is the problem that arises from a failure to address the difference between the *meaning* of a text and whether or not it is *true for us today*. To put it bluntly, questions like 'Was Jesus a feminist?' invite the rather deflating riposte, 'So what?' Even if the question about Jesus is not hopelessly anachronistic, what difference could it make to women who may be suffering oppression today to know that there are historians who believe that Jesus was a feminist? Unless we have a broad, trinitarian framework of Christian understanding and experience that enables us to see that Jesus' positive regard for women expresses something truthful about God's inclusive love, about women as made in the image of God, and about women as constituting with men the fellowship of the Church, then the supposed attitude of the historical Jesus is of hardly more than antiquarian interest.

To put it another way, unless we have an understanding of who Jesus is for us *now* and of how to be *Christ-like* in the way we as women and men conduct our relations, whether or not Jesus was a feminist is neither here nor there. This implies, in turn, that we cannot leave the task of wise readings of the Bible in the hands of historians, even historians who are Christian believers. This is not to deny that the biblical text has an historical dimension that the methods of the historian help to elucidate.[10] It is, however, to assert that historical tools are not adequate on their own for the task of discerning the truth or otherwise of the biblical testimony, including the biblical testimony about women and men in relation to God and to one another. For the question of the truth of the Bible is above all a *theological and practical* question. As Robert Morgan puts it: 'all Scripture has a literal meaning, but it does not all have a Christian theological meaning'.[11]

## Starting somewhere else: the horizon of the reader

If there is any force in these objections to approaches that start with the Bible, the alternative is that we start somewhere else: with *the horizon of the reader*. If we start with 'what the Bible says', the possibilities for disagreement are almost endless, and the answers we come up with – especially if they disturb beliefs and practices that we take for granted – can usually be postponed or kept at arm's length. So we need to start instead with questions of a different kind, such as: 'What is our experience as women and men in Church and society today?' And, 'What kind of people do we need to be in order to interpret wisely what the

Bible says in ways that are life-giving?' In the powerful words of Janet Martin Soskice:

> What we must also ask ourselves as Christians, women as well as men, is, Has our Church made things any better, or have we colluded in silencing the already half-voiced, and in making the problems of women, 'just women's problems'? Bodies are being broken day after day on linked wheels of poverty, prostitution, sexual abuse and domestic violence. How can we map these sufferings on the broken and risen body of Christ?
> (Janet Martin Soskice, 'Women's Problems', in Andrew Walker, ed., *Different Gospels. Christian Orthodoxy and Modern Theologies* (London, SPCK, 1993), pp. 194–203, at p. 203.)

The kind of approach represented here has a number of significant benefits. For a start, it avoids the biblicism, both of a loyalist and of a critical kind, implicit in accepting the original question on its own terms. Now, it is no longer the Bible that is in the dock, but *we who ask the question* or of whom the question is asked. Also, it makes possible the recognition that the Bible is the book of the Church and that adequate interpretation of the Bible will be interpretation that is played out, crafted and honed in the practice, mission, and perhaps especially in the suffering, of the Church in the world. Instead of remaining suspended at the theoretical level, the issue of whether or not the Bible is good news for women becomes an invitation and a summons to show that it is so – or can become so by the way we live and the kinds of community we build.

One important consequence of this approach is that the way the Bible is interpreted will be affected by considerations of context. The communities for whom the Bible is Christian Scripture will have the demanding task of working out in practice how the Bible is, and can be, good news for women. They will do this each in their own way, but it will not be a case of 'anything goes'. The Church, as in a fundamental sense the privileged interpreter of the Bible, provides structures of authority and traditions of interpretation and liturgical action within which to work and upon which to build.

Another and related consequence is that individual groups and communities will have to *accept responsibility* for the way they interpret and 'perform' what the Bible says about women. This will involve making decisions (either explicitly or implicitly) of a theological and ethical kind – questions about who we are and what kind of people we ought to be in relation to God and to our neighbours. Here, it will undoubtedly be the case that the communities who do this most wisely will be the ones whose members are trained in the Christian virtues and who therefore have the traditions, skills and practice necessary to the task.

The question 'Is the Bible good news for women?' is, in other words, not best taken as a question of the Bible only. Rather, it constitutes a challenge to the Church at the fundamental level of *practical spirituality*. It is those who know in what just and loving Christian practice consists who will be best equipped to read the Bible in a life-giving and liberating way. It is those who are themselves transformed and being transformed according to the image of Christ who will be best able to 'perform the Scriptures' in ways that bring transformation for women and men – and for all God's creatures.[12]

## *Putting it into practice: the two horizons*

However, the question remains, 'What difference does this emphasis on "the horizon of the reader" make to how we handle difficult texts?' What would we say if we were on the committee handling Anne Spicer's complaint about the Bible as an obscene publication which ought to be banned? On what basis might we want to say (as Christians do) that the Bible *is*, in some funda-mental sense, good news for women?

As will be clear by now, there is no simple answer! But there are a number of ways forward, all of which require *the bringing together of the two horizons* of the reader-in-community and the text of the Bible in creative and life-giving ways. For example, one strategy is to make more visible the women of the Bible. This approach serves a number of ends. It helps to counteract deep-rooted tendencies down the ages to render 'invisible' women of faith. It helps to bring to our attention the parts that Spirit-inspired women played – sometimes parts of considerable prominence – in the life of Israel, the mission of Jesus and the life of the early Church. It also provides stories with which women of faith today may be able to identify in special ways.

This is the kind of work that Elisabeth Schüssler Fiorenza does in her book *In Memory of Her*. In a quite thorough-going way, Fiorenza demonstrates that the story of Jesus and the Church is the story of women as well as men. Consider, for example, her account of the characterization of the male and female disciples in the Gospel of Mark, in which she shows how possible it is to make the text speak not only of women, but also *for* women as well:

> The misunderstanding and incomprehension of suffer-ing discipleship exemplified by the twelve turns into betrayal and denial in the passion narrative. Judas betrays Jesus, Peter denies him, and all the male disciples abandon him and flee into hiding. But while the circle of the twelve male disciples does not follow Jesus on his way to the cross for fear of risking their lives, the circle of women disciples exemplifies true discipleship. Throughout the Gospel Mark distinguishes between the circle of the twelve and a wider circle of disciples who, as Jesus' 'very own,' have received the mystery of the 'empire of God' (4:11). Though the twelve are identified as men ... the wider circle of disciples are not identified as males. That Mark's androcentric language functions as inclusive language now becomes apparent in the infor-mation that women disciples have followed Jesus from Galilee to Jerusalem, accompanied him on the way to the cross, and witnessed his death. Just as in the beginning of the Gospel Mark presents four leading male disciples who hear Jesus' call to discipleship, so at the end s/he presents four leading women disciples and mentions

them by name. The four women disciples – Mary of
Magdala, Mary, the daughter or wife of James the
younger, the mother of Joses, and Salome – are preemi-
nent among the women disciples who have followed
Jesus, just as Peter, Andrew, James, and John are preem-
inent among the twelve. Though the twelve have
forsaken Jesus, betrayed and denied him, the women
disciples, by contrast, are found under the cross, risking
their own lives and safety. That they are well aware of the
danger of being arrested and executed as followers of a
political insurrectionist crucified by the Romans is indicated in the remark that the women 'were looking from
afar.' They are thus characterized as Jesus' true 'rela-
tives.'

> (Elisabeth Schüssler Fiorenza, *In Memory of Her. A Feminist
> Theological Reconstruction of Christian Origins* (London, SCM,
> 1983), pp. 319–20.)

In reconstructive work like this – none of which is immune to
criticism, but all of which is built upon widely accepted historical-critical method – we see clearly the merging of the two
horizons of text and reader-in-community. Arising out of a practical wisdom informed both by the contemporary experience of
women and by faith in the gospel of liberation and new creation
in Christ, Fiorenza is able to show that there is another side to
the biblical witness than the one that caused Anne Spicer so
much anxiety.[13]

But Anne Spicer's concern is too profound to be dealt with
only by pointing out that there is another side to the story! Even
if, taken as a whole, the Bible points in a different direction, she
still has a point. It is a point fully acknowledged by Fiorenza
herself who, in the same book, also shows that running through
the testimony of the New Testament and other early Christian
sources there are two trajectories. On the one hand, there is a
trajectory of liberation, in which women share with men in an
inclusive 'discipleship of equals'. On the other, there is a patriarchal trajectory (reflected especially in the household codes,

certain Pauline texts and the Pastoral Epistles) where modified, but still traditional, hierarchical gender codes are put in place in a 'Christianized' form.

According to Fiorenza, only the first of the two trajectories has continuing significance as a norm for today because only this trajectory of liberation fully expresses the transformative power of the Christian gospel. But she is quite clear also that, historically speaking, by the end of the first century the trajectory of the patriarchal household code was in the ascendant so far as orthodox Christianity was concerned. This is why the 'subversive memory' of early Christian women has to be recovered. It is also why Fiorenza argues that it is a mistake to read the New Testament as if its teaching on, say, sex and gender relations provides static archetypes valid for all time. What it provides instead are historical *prototypes* in constant need of revision and reworking in the light of Christian wisdom today, itself informed by Scripture, tradition, reason and experience.

It is noteworthy, however, that Anne Spicer's point is about the offensiveness to women of certain Old Testament texts in particular. In precisely this connection, it is worth mentioning the work of another biblical scholar, Phyllis Trible. Her books, *God and the Rhetoric of Sexuality* (Philadelphia, Fortress Press, 1978) and *Texts of Terror* (London, SCM, 1992), are also an exercise in making women visible; but whereas Fiorenza combines a Christian feminist horizon with historical criticism to interpret the New Testament, Trible combines a Christian feminist horizon with literary criticism to interpret the Old Testament.

The first book is a search for the 'lost coin' (cf. Luke 15.8) of female imagery and motifs within the predominantly male language of the Old Testament, and focuses on the story of the Garden of Eden, the erotic poetry of the Song of Songs, and the 'human comedy' of the story of Naomi and Ruth. This is an exercise in recovery and retrieval that succeeds well in bringing to the fore elements of the tradition long neglected, but of particular significance for revealing female 'countervoices' in a predominantly male-oriented text.

Her second book has a much darker theme, the 'texts of

terror' from the Old Testament which tell of women abused and victimized: Hagar, the Egyptian slave-girl cast out by Abraham (Genesis 21.9–21); Tamar, the daughter of King David raped by her brother Amnon (2 Samuel 13.1–22); the unnamed concubine raped, murdered and dismembered (Judges 19.1–30); and Jephthah's virgin daughter slain as a sacrifice as a result of her father's folly (Judges 11.29–40). The pertinence of this second book to Anne Spicer's concerns about violence to women is that it addresses them head-on, in the conviction that Scripture is a mirror that reflects all of life – not only its holiness, but its horror as well. By attending with care and sympathy to what the 'texts of terror' are saying and how they speak, we are brought face to face with the dark side of our very selves and of the faith we hold, in ways that make repentance possible. Trible's own statement of what she is trying to do through her 'close reading' of these stories is worth repeating:

> If art imitates life, scripture likewise reflects it in both holiness and horror. Reflections themselves neither mandate nor manufacture change; yet by enabling insight, they may inspire repentance. In other words, sad stories may yield new beginnings. ... As a critique of culture and faith in light of misogyny, feminism is a prophetic movement, examining the status quo, pronouncing judgment, and calling for repentance. This hermeneutic engages scripture in various ways. One approach documents the case against women. It cites and evaluates long neglected data that show the inferiority, subordination, and abuse of the female in ancient Israel and the early church. By contrast, a second approach discerns within the Bible critiques of patriarchy. It upholds forgotten texts and reinterprets familiar ones to shape a remnant theology that challenges the sexism of scripture. Yet a third approach incorporates the other two. It recounts tales of terror *in memoriam* to offer sympathetic readings of abused women. If the first perspective documents misogyny

historically and sociologically, this one appropriates the data poetically and theologically. At the same time, it continues to search for the remnant in unlikely places. Such an approach characterizes these essays. It interprets stories of outrage on behalf of their female victims in order to recover a neglected history, to remember a past that the present embodies, and to pray that these terrors shall not come to pass again. In telling sad stories, a feminist hermeneutic seeks to redeem the time.

(Phyllis Trible, *Texts of Terror* (London, SCM, 1992), pp. 2–3.)

## Conclusion

It should be plain by now that if the Bible is 'good news' for women, it is *not because the Bible is politically correct*! From the viewpoint of political correctness, the Bible is a 'problem text' of mammoth proportions. There is no escaping this dilemma, as Anne Spicer's *cri de coeur* helps us to see. That is the context in which we face the issue of biblical interpretation today.

However, this kind of issue is not new, by any means. In an earlier generation, the great New Testament scholar Rudolf Bultmann attempted to deal with the question of interpretation raised not by the problem of political correctness, but by the problem of (for want of a better phrase) 'cosmological correctness': how to enable 'modern man' to be confronted by the true 'scandal' of the gospel in a way that did not demand assent to the outmoded cosmology and mythology of the biblical writings. His solution was to deny that the truth of the gospel is bound indissolubly to an ancient world-view, and to provide a method of interpretation (which he termed 'demythologization') that allowed the deeper meanings behind the biblical mythology to come to expression. These deeper meanings have to do with an understanding of human existence; and, in the existentialist philosophy of his day, Bultmann found ready-to-hand the categories of interpretation that made possible the 'translation' of biblical myth into terms intelligible to modern man.[14]

The adequacy of Bultmann's interpretation remains a matter of ongoing debate and need not detain us here;[15] but his contribution to biblical interpretation is worth noting in the present context, on at least two counts. First, Bultmann represents a major attempt in the twentieth century to acknowledge with full seriousness the importance of the question posed in this chapter: 'What to do about "problem texts"?' In other words, we are not the first to be asking these kinds of questions and there may be a lot we can learn from the attempts to answer them made by others before us. That is why wise interpretation of the Bible does not go it alone, and the wise interpreter will pay close attention to the rich tradition of biblical interpretation in which he or she stands.[16]

Second, Bultmann's solution provides a significant model for possible ways forward. On the one hand, he recognized that the way to deal with problem texts was not to excise them (like Sir Ian McKellen) or censor them (like Anne Spicer), but to interpret them *in a larger philosophical and theological framework*: to see them in all their particularity and human limitations as acknowledging the incomprehensibility and otherness of a God whose reality no words are able to convey in ways true for all time. Related to this, Bultmann showed that responsible interpretation involves ongoing acts of engagement between the reader and the text in openness to God's justifying grace in Christ.

The true meaning of the text is never static, therefore. For the true meaning resides in the transcendent, living Word of God to whom the words of the text bear frail witness. In the faith of Christians, that reality is made known to us as we struggle to engage, in the language available to us and in the circumstances of our common life, with the text's true subject-matter. In the final analysis, political correctness is not the issue – any more than cosmological correctness or historical correctness! The real issue is coming to know God and receiving the true 'eternal' life that comes through faith in the Word made flesh.

# 8

# How Then Shall We Live?

## or

## Biblical interpretation as performance

### *Introduction*

We have had occasion more than once in the preceding chapters to raise the question, 'What constitutes wise and life-giving interpretation of a text like the Bible?' In the process, we have seen that some answers to this question are helpful to a point, but fail to do full justice to the Bible understood as *the Scriptures of the Church*. This is sometimes a result of the limits of the methods that have been developed in the critical study of the text, and sometimes it is a result of the limitations of the context in which the text is read. The aim of this chapter is to consider an approach that may offer more fruitful ways forward in understanding what is involved in interpreting the Bible as Christian Scripture.

### *Interpretation as 'performance'*

In an essay published in 1981, the liberation theologian Carlos Mesters of Brazil uses a vivid metaphor from the world of musical performance to describe what happens to biblical interpretation when its location shifts from academic 'ivory towers' to everyday life among communities of the poor and oppressed. This is how he describes the contrast:

> The common people are doing something ... very important. They are reintroducing faith, community, and historical reality into the process of interpretation. When we studied the Bible back in the seminary in the

old days, we didn't have to live as a real community or really know much about reality. We didn't even have to have faith. All we needed was enough brains to understand Greek and Hebrew and to follow the professor's line of reasoning. Now the common people are helping us to realize that without faith, community, and reality we cannot possibly discover the meaning that God has put in that ancient tome for us today. Thus the common people are recovering something very important: the *sensus ecclesiae* ('sense of the church'). The community is the resonance chamber; the text is a violin string. When the people pluck the string (the biblical text), it resonates in the community and out comes the music. And that music sets the people dancing and singing.

(Carlos Mesters, 'The Use of the Bible in Christian Communities of the Common People', in S. Torres and J. Eagleson, eds., *The Challenge of Basic Christian Communities* (New York, Orbis, 1981), pp. 197–210, at pp. 208–9.)

A number of points are worthy of attention here. First, there is the assumption that true interpretation of the Bible cannot be done in a detached, 'objective', purely rational way, as if all that is required is accurate knowledge of the original languages. On the contrary, much more than this is required. This is the second important point. What is required is 'faith, community and historical reality'. Faith, because this allows the text to function as an open – indeed, inspired – text, able to speak as revelation for today. Community, because the Bible is a communal text, shaped by the communities of Synagogue and Church in order to sustain their faith-witness in an ongoing way. Historical reality, because the God to whom the text bears witness is a God who cares for us in all the particularity of our historical existence and seeks to be acknowledged in the whole of life.

This leads to the third point: that biblical interpretation is not the preserve of a cultural élite, but is the work of 'the common people'. For interpreting the Bible is not primarily a matter of

117

aesthetics or scholarship, but of faithful obedience within the life of the Church. Note, finally, the ethos that Mesters evokes: '... out comes the music. And that sets the people dancing and singing.' It is an ethos of shared vitality and joy. This reflects very well the ultimate goal of biblical interpretation: to share together in the life of God with whom the text puts us in contact, a sharing that overflows to others in true joy.

Mesters's essay is a particularly striking instance of a recent trend in discussions of the nature and goal of biblical interpretation that make use of analogies from musical and dramatic performance to help clarify what good biblical interpretation involves and how the Bible relates to worship and everyday life.

## *The roots of the idea*

The use of the metaphor of performance in biblical interpretation may be linked to at least two factors of considerable significance. The first is historical and the second is of a more theological kind.

First, there is the liturgical and worship tradition of Israel and the Church. The fact that reading the Bible has taken place from the very beginning in the context of the corporate liturgical worship, first of Israel, and subsequently of the Church, is surely significant, although not often given its due. It suggests that the art of biblical interpretation is necessarily *communal, public and participatory.* To one degree or another, the meaning of the text is something that arises out of the corporate liturgical action (or 'performance') of which it is a part and to which it contributes. Meaning, therefore, is not just a matter of what the words on the page say, but also of how the words 'speak' to readers and hearers in the context of worship and instruction within the ups and downs of everyday life and the changing circumstances of history.

This is why Dan Hardy and David Ford place a Christian understanding of the Bible and its unity firmly in the context of the practice of the praise of God in the faith communities of Israel and the Church. They put the matter this way:

The explicit praise of the Bible concentrates in itself what was most distinctive and important for Israel and, with the addition of the New Testament, for the Christian Church. Praise was the time of ultimate directness, of most active recognition of the presence and character of God. This was not just stated but also acted out, using the body as well as mind and feelings. It also focused the whole of life: everything should be subject to this God, and nothing ought to be out of harmony with this praise.

(Daniel W. Hardy and David F. Ford, *Jubilate. Theology in Praise* (London, Darton, Longman and Todd, 1984), p. 24.)

Similarly, the liturgical theologian Gordon Lathrop sees the Bible as a kind of vessel containing words that, together with water, bread and wine, constitute the central symbols of Christian liturgical action:

The assembly does not gather to a book, but to the book opened and read, turned into the source for preaching and song, perhaps made the source of visual images. The liturgy is not in books, but in lively speech set in interaction with people washing and eating and drinking.

(Gordon W. Lathrop, *Holy Things. A Liturgical Theology* (Minneapolis, Fortress Press, 1993), p. 97.)

If we turn to the Bible itself, the Psalms are an obvious example of the point we are exploring. Both the content of the Psalms (with their frequent references to the arts and instruments of performance) and their context, first in Israel's worship festivals and historical struggles, and subsequently in the worship and life of Synagogue and Church, point to the integral relation between the meaning of the words and their performance in music, song, dance and daily existence. All this is epitomized in Psalm 150:

Praise the LORD!
Praise God in his sanctuary;
praise him in his mighty firmament!
Praise him for his mighty deeds;
praise him according to his exceeding greatness!
Praise him with trumpet sound;
praise him with lute and harp!
Praise him with timbrel and dance;
praise him with strings and pipe!
Praise him with sounding cymbals;
praise him with loud clashing cymbals!
Let everything that breathes praise the LORD!
Praise the LORD!

It is not at all coincidental that the Psalter *ends* with this psalm, for it epitomizes what the Psalter as a whole wants to express and encourage. There is a sense, furthermore, in which this psalm stands for the Bible as a whole as well. Just as Psalm 150 evokes the practice of the praise of God, so the whole of Scripture has that in view also; for the purpose of Scripture is to reveal the One who as creator, redeemer and sustainer calls forth our wholehearted performance of the 'sacrifice' of praise and thanksgiving.

The other, not unrelated factor in the turn to the metaphor of performance to clarify what biblical interpretation involves comes from critical theological attention to *the kind of book the Bible is* and what it is for. As we have seen previously, because the Bible contains much historical material and can be used by historians who want to reconstruct the history of Israel or the events of Jesus' life or the history of the early Church, it is easy to assume that the Bible is only a source of historical information. This is correct as far as it goes, but does it go far enough? Does not the Bible also contain poetry and wisdom, myth and legend, law and prophecy, parable and apocalypse? And do most readers read the Bible only in order to become better informed about life in ancient Israel or at the time of Jesus? Do we not much more read the Bible for guidance, instruction and inspiration in the life of faith?

If these latter concerns are most important for us, then the only way we can test out what the Bible says is by *putting it into practice* in some way: what Nicholas Lash (as we shall see) calls 'performing the Scriptures'. To put it another way, it is one thing to find out (with the help of the historian) what the text of the Bible meant, but it is quite another to find out (in the context of faithful discipleship) what the text means for me, or us, today.

One helpful step in this direction involves the recognition that, while the Bible contains much information of historical value, nevertheless as Scripture it exists as a text-in-community where it is read or heard for instruction and inspiration. Once this is recognized, the question of validity in biblical interpretation is seen to be a more complex matter. In some ways, perhaps, it is more like judging the performance of a Shakespearean play or a piece of Beethoven than verifying points of historical reliability. On this model, the meaning and truth of the Bible are discoveries that take place as much 'in front of' the text, in the interaction between text and reader or hearer, as 'behind' the text in the discovery of points of correspondence between written word and historical event.[1]

## Specific advocates

As a way of exploring further what is at stake here, it is worth considering the two accounts which, in recent times, have made most of the 'performance' analogy.[2] The first is that of the Roman Catholic theologian Nicholas Lash in his essay 'Performing the Scriptures', a seminal essay published in 1982.[3] Here, in answer to the question as to what is involved in the interpretation of texts, Lash makes the important point that, 'for different kinds of text, different kinds of activity count as the fundamental form of their interpretation'.[4] According to Lash, among the closest analogies to biblical interpretation are the interpretation of a Beethoven score or a Shakespearean tragedy.

Thus, for the interpretation of Beethoven, it is not sufficient to be able to read the notes and play the instruments. Nor is it sufficient to know, with the help of the music historian, in what circumstances the music was composed or how the score has been interpreted orchestrally in the past. Nor is it sufficient even to play the notes of the score with technical accuracy. Of course, none of these things is to be gainsaid. Nevertheless, the central act of the interpretation of a Beethoven score is the performance, a performance that, if it is to inspire or give pleasure or console, has to be a matter of more than technical accuracy, and instead a kind of *creative fidelity* that allows the musical score to come alive again in the present moment. Important also is the recognition that this is a social or communal activity involving not just conductor and orchestra, but an audience of (more or less informed) listeners and critics as well. There is a sense in which the audience is taking part in the performance as well as the orchestra, and that what Beethoven's score 'means' arises out of the convergence of creative contributions from both orchestra and audience.

Or take the interpretation of Shakespeare – *King Lear*, for example. Once again, textual critics will be able to assist by establishing the most authentic version of the text; historians of Elizabethan times will help interpretation also by giving us a sense of the historical background of Shakespeare and his plays; and literary critics will contribute to the appreciation of the literary qualities of Shakespeare's poetry, rhetoric, characterization, and so on. But the central act of the interpretation of *King Lear* comes in the performance of the play on a stage by a company of actors in the presence of an audience.

Furthermore, the meaning of the play is not best conveyed in a performance that is technically correct, for such performances are usually judged to be 'flat' or 'lifeless' – what theatrical director Peter Brook memorably refers to as 'deadly theatre'.[5] They give the literal sense of the play without conveying its essential dynamic. On the contrary, true interpretation occurs when the performance is 'original' or 'inspired' or 'creative' in some sense, such that we feel that we have come to understand the play in a new way and perhaps even that we have come to understand ourselves in a new way as well.

These analogies help establish Lash's main point, that 'there are at least some texts that only begin to deliver their meaning in so far as they are "brought into play" through interpretative performance'. For Lash, the Bible is one such text. He states his position thus:

> I want to suggest, first, that, although the texts of the New Testament may be read, and read with profit, by anyone interested in Western culture and concerned for the human predicament, the fundamental form of the Christian interpretation of scripture is the life, activity and organization of the believing community. Secondly, that Christian practice, as interpretative action, consists in the performance of texts which are construed as 'rendering', bearing witness to, one whose words and deeds, discourse and suffering, 'rendered' the truth of God in human history. The performance of the New Testament enacts the conviction that these texts are most appropriately read as the story of Jesus, the story of every-one else, and the story of God.
>
> (Nicholas Lash, *Theology on the Way to Emmaus* (London, SCM, 1986), p. 42.)

The implications of Lash's 'performance' model of biblical interpretation are profound. Among other things, it suggests that inquiry into the meaning of the Bible is inadequate if it is not at the same time an inquiry into its truth – that is to say, an inquiry into whether or not creative fidelity as to what the text is about *makes human transformation possible.*

It also suggests that the art of biblical interpretation is not primarily something abstract and theoretical, a matter of private judgement only, to be consumed according to taste. Rather, it is something practical, personal, communal and political: to do with changing and being changed according to the image of the risen Christ whose story the Bible tells. As with the interpreta-tion of music and drama, the meaning of the Bible is discovered and expressed in patterns of human action, for that is the only way a text like the Bible is appropriately 'brought into play'.

The other account to look at is that of the Methodist theologian and patristic scholar Frances Young, in her recent book, *The Art of Performance* (London, Darton, Longman and Todd, 1990). Like Nicholas Lash, Young addresses the problem of how to appropriate the Bible in the modern world: 'How can we treat the Bible as Holy Scripture if it is to be subjected to literary or historical criticism like any other book? ... How can we live in and worship with the Bible ... in a modern world so different from the past which produced and used it?' Young's answer is that the way we can do so is illuminated by study of the way the early Church Fathers interpreted the Bible, especially if we see what they did in the light of the analogy of musical performance. Her basic point is that the relationship between the text of the Bible and the interpreter ought to be understood by analogy with the relationship between a musical score and the musician.

The analogy is worked out in a number of areas. For example, in the first chapter Young suggests that true interpretation of the Bible is a matter *more of theology than of method.* For her own theology of Scripture, she invokes the 'two natures' doctrine of classic Chalcedonian christology and argues that the Bible likewise can be thought of as having 'two natures': the Word of God and human words historically conditioned. How this can be so is then argued for by analogy with music, which also, it is suggested, has 'two natures':

> It is of the essence of music that it is a 'language' embodied in physical reality, and yet an analytical account of soundwaves in the air, resonances and intervals, vibrating strings, reeds or membranes comes nowhere near providing an 'exegesis' of it. Music moves through time, change and development, rhythm as well as melody, being of its essence; yet paradoxically we may speak of time standing still or of experiencing 'timelessness' when caught up in its 'higher' or 'deeper' reality. This 'spiritual nature' is incarnate in a medium of which

'physics' can give an account both explanatory and necessarily reductive, yet it is not translatable into any other medium, except by way of analogy: what music 'means' cannot be expressed in words without change and loss. In order to communicate, music has to be 'realised' through performance and interpretation. ... The Biblical Canon, then, is as it were the repertoire, inherited, given, to be performed. Selections are performed day by day and week by week in the liturgy. Exegetes, like musicians, need the discipline of rehearsing the score, trying out ways of interpretation, researching the possibilities of meaning, grappling with the 'physical' or 'historical' constraints of the language, preparing for performance with appropriate ornamentation. ... But all preachers and congregations are the performers and hearers on whose inspiration the communication of the Word of God depends. That Word is both 'incarnate' in a time-bound text and yet eternal, transcending the limits of human language and culture.

(Frances Young, *The Art of Performance* (London, Darton, Longman and Todd, 1990), pp. 22, 25.)

This suggestion that the Bible and music are fundamentally alike in both having 'two natures' that find expression in the art of 'performance' provides the background for her development of the analogy in other ways. What she says in chapter 2 of *The Art of Performance* about the phenomenon of the biblical canon is a case in point. The canon of Scripture, encompassing a small library of individual works whose literary genre varies widely, is best understood by analogy with a classic repertoire in music or drama. Thus, the formation of the biblical canon within the respective communities of Israel and the Church is like the rather mysterious process of sifting which brings a classic repertoire of music into being. What is included is judged as having a significance that is epoch-making in some way and of more than passing worth. It is material that does not wear thin with repetition, but is able to speak beyond the circumstances in and for which it was originally composed.

Furthermore, just as interpretation of the repertoire has to take account of the diversity of musical genres of which it is composed, so too biblical interpretation has to take account of the diversity of literary genres encompassed by the Bible. Like the classic repertoire in music or drama, the Bible – in all its diversity and complexity, and with a history of interpretation that must itself be influential in judging how it ought to be interpreted – is a fundamental resource for the life of a community. In the act of authentic performance, the community is both *constituted and transformed.*

Among other striking applications of the musical performance analogy, Young's final chapter (chapter 8), 'Improvisation and Inspiration' is worth mentioning also. Here she suggests that the best way to think of the process whereby the ancient biblical text is allowed to speak today as Scripture is by analogy with cadenzas in concertos. Individual 'performances' of Scripture in preaching and teaching are like the improvisation of the performer of the cadenza. There is the need for faithfulness to the style and themes of the concerto, but also virtuosity and inspiration in developing these in ways fitting both to the music and to the occasion. So too with 'performance' of the Bible and the question of what to make of pluralism in biblical interpretation:

> The orchestra is the community of the faithful. ...
> Ultimately the audience is the world. Just playing the old
> classic without a cadenza is like reading the lessons
> without a sermon. ... In order to improvise these essen-
> tial new cadenzas, which will essentially be somewhat
> ephemeral, the preacher needs skills, philological skills,
> hermeneutical theories, imaginative insights, and a lot of
> sensitivity to context. The bridge [of communication]
> has to be flexible or it will crack under pressure.
> (Frances Young, *The Art of Performance* (London, Darton,
> Longman and Todd, 1990), pp. 161–2.)

## *Further reflections on interpretation as 'performance'*

It is important to remember that any analogy is likely to be helpful only to a point and can be taken too far. What is most helpful about the performance analogy is that it forces us to recognize that the interpretation of a text depends on the kind of text being interpreted, and that the biblical text shares with musical scores and texts of drama the fact that adequate interpretation requires their being 'brought into play' in patterns of human action of one kind or another.

It is not enough to establish the intentions of the original author or composer, even if it were possible to do so. Nor is it enough to determine the historical circumstances, audience, and so on that may have influenced the process of composition and its substance. Such tasks are important for those whose job is that of criticism; and they have become areas of immense technical expertise. But the analogy from musical and dramatic performance helps us to see that *the Bible is mute* until it engages and is engaged by a community of people seeking to know God truly and to be transformed into the image of God. To repeat Carlos Mesters's words, cited at the outset:

> ... the common people are recovering something very important: the *sensus ecclesiae* ('sense of the church'). The community is the resonance chamber; the text is a violin string. When the people pluck the string (the biblical text), it resonates in the community and out comes the music. And that music sets the people dancing and singing.

On the other hand, it would be a mistake to overlook an important difference between interpreting a score of music and interpreting the Bible. One way of characterizing this difference is to say that 'performance' is a slippery word! The kind of performance involved in playing Beethoven's symphonies or in acting out *King Lear* is significantly different from what it might mean to 'perform the Scriptures'. All involve patterns of human action in a communal context. However, in music and drama the canons of judgement are primarily aesthetic, and those who make the judgements tend to be a cultural élite. In relation to performing the Scriptures, on the other hand, the canons of judgement are primarily theological, christological and ethical, and adequacy of 'performance' is the concern of the community as a whole.

On this last point, Liberation Theology in particular has helped us to see that true interpretation is inseparable from the struggle for personal and social justice, and that it is often those who are on the margins of society, not the cultural élite, who are best able to judge what constitutes adequate 'performance' of the Scriptures. This is the special force of Carlos Mesters's work on the interpretation of the Bible in the basic Christian communities of Latin America.[6]

Maybe it is significant in this regard that Frances Young's study has no chapter on something like 'The Bible and Ethics'. It is as if the musical performance analogy exhausts itself at this point. A clue in the same direction comes from Nicholas Lash's observation that, unlike performing Beethoven or Shakespeare, the kind of human activity involved in performing the Scriptures is *a full-time affair*. This is so, he says, 'because it consists in their enactment as the social existence of an entire human community. ... The performance of scripture is the life of the church.'[7]

Once we recognize this crucial point, then it is important to leave the musical performance analogy behind. Or perhaps we should say that the musical performance analogy needs to be allowed to stand alongside those analogies more suited to the exploration of other aspects of what is involved in interpreting Scripture for Christian discipleship.

## Conclusion: by way of example – the temptation of Jesus

In drawing this chapter to a close, however, it is important to illustrate what biblical interpretation as performance might look like in practice. This is where the line between theology and biography becomes blurred. That is to say, the performance model draws to our attention the fact that the best commentaries on the Bible are not books, but *the lives* of those individuals and communities that manifest the transforming power of God encountered in Scripture.[8]

This is why the Bible is full of stories of men and women in their relationships with one another and with God. The best example is Jesus himself, whose story is told four times, foretold at other points, and imitated at yet others. Nor may it be coincidental that, according to the Gospels, Jesus did not write any texts or any commentaries on Scripture. In fact, the only reference to Jesus writing is in the story of the adulterous woman, where Jesus writes with his finger on the ground (John 8.6) – and John does not even tell us what he wrote! What we find instead is a whole life *inscribed by Scripture* and lived out in accordance with Scripture. Jesus interpreted Scripture by 'performing' the will of God in a life of obedience as God's 'Son'.

The story of the temptation (Matthew 4.1–11) is a classic instance.[9] Three times the devil tests Jesus' loyalty to his heavenly Father, even quoting Scripture in order to lead Jesus astray. But Jesus remains faithful. He refuses to allow even the authoritative text of Scripture to subvert his loyalty to the God of Scripture, for that would be to confuse the words of the text with the reality of God beyond the text. In essence, what the devil tries repeatedly to do is to get Jesus to betray his calling (confirmed at his baptism) as God's obedient Son by going about it the devil's way rather than God's. However, as this story and the Gospel as a whole show, Jesus 'performs' the Scriptures in a way that is true to his calling as God's 'beloved Son'.

The first temptation or testing is to use his power as the Son of God to feed himself, for he has after all been fasting for forty days and nights (4.2f.). But Jesus knows that his calling is not to meet his own needs, for that would be an abuse of his relationship with his heavenly Father. His duty, rather, is to trust in the Father who cares for us more than we know and who gives us our daily bread (6.11, 25–33). His duty also is to meet the needs of others, in fulfilment of the love commandment (5.43–8; 22.34–40). This is what he in fact does when he feeds the hungry multitudes (twice!), later on in the story (14.13–21; 15.32–9). So, unlike the Israel of old, which tested God by demanding food in the wilderness, Jesus, the embodiment of the true Israel, shows when he is tested that feeding on the word of God is what is necessary (4.3–4).

If the first temptation is for Jesus to doubt divine providence by providing bread for himself, the second is for Jesus to test divine providence by forcing God's hand through the precipitate action of throwing himself off the pinnacle of the temple. But although the devil can quote the Scriptures (cf. Psalm 91.11–12) as a warrant for what he wants Jesus to do, Jesus knows that to 'perform the Scriptures' truly is to act in a way that does not presume on providence by putting God to the test (cf. Deuteronomy 6.16). It is, rather, to trust that the Father will save the Son in accordance with the Father's will – and that is neither to be questioned nor presumed upon. Being God's true Son is not a matter of having a self-assurance based upon miraculous feats. As the story of Jesus unfolds, it is shown to be something quite different: not throwing himself off the temple pinnacle, nor calling on angelic intervention (26.53–4), nor taking himself down from the cross (27.40, 42), but allowing himself to be betrayed, tried and condemned to death at the hands of his enemies in fulfilment of the Father's will (26.36–46).

The third temptation is yet another temptation to doubt God's providence and to transfer allegiance to someone else. For the devil offers Jesus a short-cut to glory by offering him the reward of (apparently) universal authority if he will acknowledge the devil as supreme rather than the Father in heaven. But instead of accepting the earthly kingdoms offered him now by the devil, Jesus shows his trust in the Father to reward him at the end, after he has fulfilled the Father's will. This means going the 'narrow' way of the cross; but at the resurrection, the risen Christ shows his disciples that his trust in the Father has not been misplaced. For now, 'All authority on heaven and on earth has been given to me'; and instead of having given his worship to the devil, it is Christ who now receives worship from those who are his (cf. 28.16–20).

130

Jesus, in the faith of Christians, is the supreme example of what it means to 'perform the Scriptures'. He is so because as the Son of God he had true discernment of the Father's will and remained obedient to it. Likewise, our vocation, as sons and daughters of God, is to perform the Scriptures. To do this faithfully is to follow the example of the Son in the power of the Spirit.

# 9

## The Bible For The Common Good

or

## Community in 1 Corinthians

### *Introduction*

'Performing the Scriptures' is not just something we do as individuals; there is a strong communal dimension as well. That is why this final chapter is called 'The Bible for the Common Good'. Taking as our case-study Paul's First Letter to the Corinthians, we will begin to see how significant that communal dimension is in the Bible and how powerful is the challenge it offers to Christians in the (post-)modern world.

But why choose 1 Corinthians? First, because we have not had much to say about St Paul thus far, so this is a chance to fill an important gap. Second, because 1 Corinthians is a letter to an identifiable early Christian community in a pluralistic, urban setting similar, in some ways, to that in which many of us live today. Third, because the main focus of its concerns is to do with how to live together in unity as 'the body of Christ'. Fourth, because 1 Corinthians addresses with considerable sophistication the question of the relation between the Church and the world. And finally, because in the letter Paul's apostolic autobiography is related to his moral exhortation in a way that is instructive, especially for questions of leadership and authority in the community.

In addition, many readers of 1 Corinthians will testify to the fact that here is a text that speaks across the centuries to our contemporary concerns in a way that appears remarkably prescient – as if we are all Corinthians![1] What Paul says resonates, for example, with the concerns addressed by Jonathan Sacks in his Reith Lectures for 1990, in which he highlights a number of serious threats to our social fabric: economic individualism, moral pluralism and the privatization of values, the loss of institutions that sustain communities of memory and character, the shift from a traditional duty-based ethic to a secular rights-based ethic, the tendency of the religions to polarize into extremes of liberalism or conservatism, and so on.[2] In the light of such threats, Sacks calls for the renewal of community, both at the local level of families, churches and voluntary associations, and at the national level of society now reconceived (but rather too vaguely) as a 'community of communities'. Towards the end of his final lecture, he says:

> We have run up against the limits of a certain view of human society: one that believed that progress was open-ended, that there was no limit to economic growth, that conflict always had a political solution, and that all solutions lay with either the individual or the state. We will search, as we have already begun to do, for an ethical vocabulary of duties as well as rights; for a new language of environmental restraint; for communities of shared responsibility and support; for relationships more enduring than those of temporary compatibility; and for that sense, that lies at the heart of the religious experience, that human life has meaning beyond the self.
>
> (Jonathan Sacks, *The Persistence of Faith. Religion, Morality and Society in a Secular Age* (London, Weidenfeld and Nicolson, 1991), p. 92.)

In the sentence that follows, he adds: 'These are themes central to the great religious traditions, and we will not have to re-invent them.' Quite so. Indeed, within the Christian scriptural tradition, many of these themes come together, and are addressed (at least by implication or analogy), in 1 Corinthians, as we shall see.

## The word of the cross and the transformation of community

Paul's First Letter to the Corinthians is written with a view to restoring order and unity in a community seriously threatened by division and factionalism. This concern surfaces at the beginning of the letter (1.10ff.) and unites the letter as a whole.[3] It is not the case that chapters 1 to 4 deal with the problem of religiously motivated party strife, and chapters 5 to 16 with a conglomeration of loosely related pastoral and theological challenges facing the Church. Rather, the common denominator that ties all the issues together is that they all contribute to centrifugal forces that threaten the unity and identity of the Church – and therefore its very existence.

Fundamental to Paul's response is the strategy of what we might call (irrespective of its associations in current British politics!) 'back to basics'. Most notably, where the baptismal ritual of entry into church membership appears to have been open to subversion into a ritual of entry to a particular church *faction*, Paul counters by reminding the Corinthians of the power of God made available to them by the preaching of 'the cross of Christ': 'For Christ did not send me to baptize but to preach the gospel, and not with eloquent wisdom, lest the cross of Christ be emptied of its power' (1.17). This recalls the Corinthians to the inaugurating word of revelation that they share in common. It also recalls them to Paul himself as the apostle who came as the messenger of revelation and to whom, therefore, they owe common allegiance as their spiritual 'father' (4.14–21). Gospel word and gospel messenger belong together, the implication being that to depart from one is to depart from the other also.

But Paul's words are a reminder of something else as well. They are a reminder of the basic *transformation of life* that the revelation of the power of God in the cross of Christ makes possible: 'but to those who are called, both Jews and Greeks, Christ the power of God and the wisdom of God' (1.24). That short phrase, 'both Jews and Greeks', speaks volumes. It expresses the universal scope of the saving revelation and the call to embody

134

that in a transformed pattern of common life where the lines of purity are drawn no longer according to ethnicity (cf. 10.32; 12.11), and where the lines of human worth are drawn no longer in relation to rank and status in the world-at-large (1.26–9). Instead, God has acted in sovereign, creative love and brought into being a new, eschatological humanity: '[God] is the source of your life in Christ Jesus, whom God made our wisdom, our righteousness and sanctification and redemption' (1.30). What has such potential for creating divisions old and new – conflicting notions of 'wisdom', divergence over what constitutes 'righteousness', and so on – is focused back again on the revelation of God in Christ and his cross.

What all this implies is that, for Paul, Christian community is both a response to, and a participation in, divine grace. This grace has a particularity about it – it is a heavenly 'secret' (*mustē-rion*) now made known – and that particularity defines the identity of both the apostle who imparts it and the community who receives it. Thus, because God's revelation is cruciform, the life of the apostle and the ethos and identity of the community are to be cruciform also. The authority of the apostle and the unity of the Church arise out of their faithfulness, in the power of God's Spirit, to this revelation in all its particularity. What undermines apostolic authority and threatens church unity is summed up in the term 'to boast'. It is 'boasting', along with the associated competition for honour, status and power, which blind humanity to the hidden wisdom of God revealed in Christ (cf. 2.8) and sow the seeds of a competitive social order oriented on violence, domination and intolerance of the weak. But in Christ, a new community is called into being, and 'boasting' is transformed from violence into doxology: 'Let him who boasts, boast of the Lord' (1.31; cf. 3.21; 4.7).

## *The Lord's Supper and the Church as a community of memory*

We ought not to be surprised in reading 1 Corinthians to discover that Paul's preaching of the cross and the related practice of baptism in the name of Christ raised as many problems as it solved. The bringing to birth of a new humanity and transformed patterns of common life would not be authentic if they did not involve pain, struggle and conflict. This is the case for Paul himself: 'When reviled, we bless; when persecuted, we endure; when slandered, we try to conciliate; we have become, and are now, as the refuse of the world, the offscouring of all things' (4.13). So why should it be different for Paul's churches? The point is made powerfully by Fred Craddock:

> It is naïve to think one can function with the simple formula: People have problems and the gospel resolves them. The fact is, the gospel generates in individual lives and in society a new set of problems. One has only to love impartially and hatred is threatened and stirred to violence. One has only to speak the truth and falsehood takes the stand with pleasing lies. Invite persons of different social and economic backgrounds around the same table and the fellowship is strained, often breaking apart. Announce freedom in Christ Jesus and some turn a deaf ear to the call for restraint for the sake of the weaker brother or sister. Place in church leadership persons who have never led in any other arena and arrogance often replaces service. Plant the cross in a room and the upwardly mobile convert it into a ladder. Evil, by whatever name it is called, will not sit idly by and allow the gospel to transform a community.
> (Fred B. Craddock, 'Preaching to Corinthians',
> *Interpretation*, vol. XLIV (1990), p. 167.)

If evil does not sit idly by when Paul preaches the cross and people are baptized into Christ, neither does it restrain itself when people try to embody and consolidate their new identity around a shared table and a common meal. Now, the tendency to convert the cross into a social ladder and baptism into a ritual of status differentiation carries over into that most crucial of rituals of solidarity in antiquity, table fellowship around a meal:

'... when you assemble as a church, I hear that there are divisions among you; ... For in eating, each one goes ahead with his own meal, and one is hungry and another is drunk. What! Do you not have houses to eat and drink in? Or do you despise the church of God and humiliate those who have nothing?' (11.18,21–2).

This is a revealing accusation.[4] On the positive side, it shows that people from a wide range of social backgrounds are coming together: for some have plenty and others have nothing; some have leisure enough to be able to arrive early and others are in servitude and arrive late (cf. 11.33). On the negative side, however, the accusation shows that, instead of functioning as a practical and symbolic focus of life-transforming unity, the meal bears all too many of the marks of the competition for dominance brought into the Church from the household, the voluntary association and the city-state: hence the conspicuous consumption, the eating apart, and the attempt to exercise influence by bestowing honour on some and shame on others. The Church was offering its own version of the imperial 'bread and circuses'.

If we ask how things could have degenerated so, we are forced to reckon with a number of considerations. First, it seems clear that the process of resocialization that began with conversion and baptism into Christ was slow and uncertain, due, not least, to the power of inherited cultural mores and social reflexes and to the pervasiveness of alternative models of sociability in the wider environment. Given that believers were now living in two social worlds simultaneously, and that Paul wanted to discourage moves to withdraw from the pagan world (cf. 5.10; 7.12–16), the danger that the community of saints would be contaminated by the old ways remained strong. This is likely to have been the case, especially in the more 'ingrained' ritual or ceremonial areas of life like temple worship, marriage ties and sexual relations, and meals public and private.

Second – and what I want to draw particular attention to here – it also seems clear that the Christian community at Corinth was a group *short on shared narrative and corporate memory*.[5] Among other things, it appears that its members (especially the prominent ones) so exalted individual 'spiritual' experience that they neglected shared engagement with the Scriptures and the apostolic tradition, and played down the importance of the more didactic gifts of prophetic discernment and teaching (cf. 12.7ff., 28–30; 14.1ff.). This helps to explain why Paul, in this very act of epistolary communication, adopts the role of a father instructing his spiritual offspring (4.14–21). It also explains why, at crucial points, he *reminds* the Corinthians of both dominical and scriptural tradition that he has passed on to them previously, but that they seem to have forgotten or misconstrued or remembered only selectively (cf. 15.1ff.).

The Last Supper tradition is one such point (11.23ff.; cf. 10.14–22). Having castigated the Corinthians for their abuse of table fellowship, he recalls them from eating their 'own' meals to participating together in the 'Lord's meal', informed by authoritative tradition received 'from the Lord' and 'handed on' to them by the apostle himself. What is especially striking here is the way in which, as with the ritual of baptism early on in the letter, apostolic tradition is introduced as a control and a corrective. It is as if the non-verbal communication that takes place in the ritualized behaviour of the meal is so powerfully expressive and yet also so open to a variety of construals – some of which can be destructive and divisive – that an accompanying authoritative communication of a verbal kind is required. The food for thought embodied in the meal requires for its interpretation the food for thought embodied in the apostolic tradition. If you like, word and sacrament: where the word situates the meal and those who eat it in a community of memory and shared narrative.

Significantly, that narrative is part of the same narrative introduced at the letter's beginning: Christ crucified. Says Paul: 'For as often as you eat this bread and drink the cup, you proclaim the Lord's death until he comes' (11.26). So the narrative of Christ crucified is intended by Paul to be the constant point of reference. It is what imparts the power for a new pattern of common life at the start, and it is what imparts the power for consolidating that common life as it goes on. By repeatedly drawing it to their attention and by insisting that their regular gatherings for the meal serve to proclaim it, Paul, the good teacher, is impressing indelibly on their corporate memory both what has brought them to life and what will sustain that life in harmony.

## Holiness, discipline and the Church as a community of character

If the Christian community at Corinth was short on shared narrative and corporate memory, it appears also, and as a corollary, to have been lacking in discipline – so much so that the unity and integrity of the community were at risk.[6] Paul's letter gives evidence of a divisive rivalry working itself out in a number of ways: the exercise of patronage, the practice of 'boasting' and other forms of self-display, and the destructive distribution of honour and shame. The letter also gives evidence of spiritual immaturity, lack of discernment in basic areas of social intercourse, the exaltation of individual liberty over communal responsibility, and a dangerous naïvety about personal authority and the limits of the religious community. The relative absence of a shared narrative reiterated in common worship and reinforced by communal discipline meant that the resources for building a *community of character* were in short supply.

Paul's response takes a number of forms.[7] First, he uses a particular kind of language. This is the language of holiness understood as separation and discrimination, a language available to him already from the Jewish moral tradition. Noteworthy, for example, is the designation of the addressees at the very beginning of the letter: 'To the *church of God* which is at Corinth, to those *sanctified in Christ Jesus, called to be saints* together with all those who in every place *call on the name* of our Lord Jesus Christ ...' (1.2) (added emphasis). There could be no clearer expression of Paul's intention to refocus the Corinthians' self-understanding on their authentic, common vocation to be God's holy people, united under the lordship of Christ. The same could be said of his use of the language of divine election (e.g. 1.26ff.), the language of servitude or indebtedness to God, Christ or the Spirit (e.g. 3.5–23), and the pervasive language of fictive kinship to designate believers as 'brothers' and 'sisters', members together of the household of God.

Corresponding with this language of separation used of insiders is the language used of outsiders. They are 'the pagans', 'the world', 'those outside', 'the unrighteous', 'the immoral', 'unbelievers' and 'idolaters' – to mention just the most prominent terms in the lexicon of holiness upon which Paul draws (cf. 5–6; 7.12ff.; 10.7; etc.). Such terms are intended by Paul to reinforce the Corinthian believers' (apparently rather weak or confused) sense of belonging to a new, redeemed humanity. They offer the Corinthians a traditional, rhetorically powerful linguistic resource by means of which both to think about themselves differently and to see themselves as being different.

As well as the language of separation, there is Paul's insistence on moral and social discipline in the community. Thus, because the acceptance and exercise of discipline requires the acknowledgement of authority in the community, Paul asserts the legitimacy of his own apostolic authority over the community as its founder, father, nurturer and principal model. But he does not stop with that. He also imparts a countervailing 'wisdom' to that being propagated by those he views as trouble-makers. He demands the renunciation of habits of speech and action that promote faction rather than unity. He introduces principles and rules for the orderly and seemly governance of members' social relations, including instructions on who to eat with and who to sleep with. Under the guiding christological metaphor of 'the body of Christ', he gives instructions on the proper conduct of Christian meetings. And, in order to maximize the possibility of unity in a community with so much potential and actual diversity, he advocates an overriding ethic of humility and other-regarding love (*agapē*). All this he does in a powerful act of theological persuasion which seeks to situate the lives of the Corinthians in an eschatological perspective: between the cross, at the letter's opening, and the resurrection, towards the letter's end. It is the cross and resurrection of Christ that has gained for the Corinthians participation in the kingdom of God; and Paul's desire is to see that participation embodied in the life of the community.

I use the word 'embodied' advisedly, because it is striking how much of Paul's instruction in communal discipline has to do with members' bodies – above all, in two areas of bodily activity: eating and issues of commensality on the one hand, and sexual intercourse and issues related to marriage and gender-roles on the other.[8] From a social anthropological perspective, this is not surprising. In her well-known study, *Natural Symbols*, Mary Douglas has shown that 'the human body is always treated as an image of society',[9] and that concerns about the boundaries of the social body tend to be expressed in anxiety about the boundaries of its members' physical bodies. The body's orifices are a special focus of attention in this regard, especially the mouth and the sexual organs. Rules, norms and customs for ordering and guarding the orifices of individual, physical bodies are a powerful practical and symbolic way of ordering and guarding the boundaries of the social body.

So what Paul says about food and sex are not disparate concerns from a vague catalogue of problems, as if Paul is a kind of first-century 'agony aunt'! Rather, there is an underlying socio-logic, itself related to an even more fundamental theo-logic. In short, Paul is talking about three kinds of 'body', not just one: the believer's physical body cannot be understood independently of the social body of the Church, and the Church cannot be understood appropriately except as 'the body of Christ'. Acknowledging this interrelationship of three kinds of body is important. It helps us to see, for example, that Paul's sexual ethics are an integral part of his social ethics, and that his social ethics (which touch on a range of issues much wider than just sex) are an integral part of belonging to Christ under the sovereignty of God in the power of the Spirit.

To take one example: in addressing a case of sexual immorality, where certain members are attending meals as guests at pagan temples and having recourse to the prostitutes there

(6.12ff.; cf. 1 Corinthians 8—10), Paul insists that food, sex and the body are not immaterial to the life of freedom in the kingdom of God. On the contrary, true freedom is shown in doing what is advantageous to others (6.12a), what demonstrates God's resurrection power in the life of the individual (6.14), what expresses being part of Christ's body, the Church (6.15), and what shows the believer's new identity as a 'temple of the Holy Spirit' (6.19). Paul says:

> The body is not meant for immorality, but for the Lord, and the Lord for the body. And God raised the Lord and will also raise us up by his power. Do you not know that your bodies are members of Christ? Shall I therefore take the members of Christ and make them members of a prostitute? Never! ... Do you not know that your body is a temple of the Holy Spirit within you, which you have from God? You are not you own; you were bought with a price. So glorify God in your body (6.13b–20).

Striking in Paul's argument here is the way the freedom of the individual is reinterpreted by being set firmly in a wider context of significance and obligation – in the context of a solidarity whose members are not just earthly but heavenly as well. For Paul, uniting with others is a legitimate expression of freedom only if it is a union of the right kind. Union with a prostitute is wrong and disorderly because it contradicts the most important union of all: with the Lord and with the Lord's people. In arguing thus, it is noteworthy that allusion to the shared narrative of Christ's cross and resurrection recurs once more and that Paul's incipiently trinitarian theo-logic comes powerfully to the fore to provide the framework for moral discernment and action.

## The body of Christ and the Church as an alternative society

The metaphor of the Church as 'the body of Christ', introduced briefly in the instructions on avoiding sexual immorality just discussed (cf. 6.15), is developed more fully later on, not least in 1 Corinthians 12.12–31. If in 1 Corinthians 6, the body of Christ is a way of situating and controlling individual bodies in their sexual relations, and if in 1 Corinthians 10—11, it is a way of situating and controlling individual bodies in their eating practices, in 1 Corinthians 12 the body of Christ is a way of situating and controlling individual bodies in their life together as the people of God, a life given primary focus in communal worship.

If we ask what it is about the metaphor that allows it to function this way in 1 Corinthians 12, attention needs to be drawn to the fact that, in ancient political literature, the body was a common metaphor for society or the state, frequently used as a rhetorical means both to combat discord and to encourage unity in diversity.[10] This 'political' dimension of the metaphor is easily overlooked if 'the body of Christ' is understood in purely eucharistic terms or if what Paul says in 1 Corinthians 12 and 14 is segregated from the underlying preoccupation of the letter as a whole by too narrow a focus on 'early Christian worship' or on things 'charismatic'. But once we take with full seriousness Paul's underlying preoccupation with combating factionalism and establishing order and unity in the Church at Corinth, and once we surrender modernist tendencies to separate politics from religion or worship from everyday life, we are more likely to recognize that the argument in these chapters represents another step in Paul's attempt to establish the Church as an *alternative society* autonomous in essential respects from the society-at-large.

This is consistent with Paul's use of the language of separation already noted. It is consistent also with his condemnation of the practice of resolving intramural disputes (probably over marriage, property and inheritance) in the public courts (6.1–11), and of joining in meals at pagan temples presided over by demons (10.1–22). Nor is it coincidental that Paul uses the metaphors of plant, building and temple as designations of the Church (e.g. 3.6ff., 10ff., 16–17), for these are also biblical metaphors used of the sacred polity of Israel. It is very likely that 'the body of Christ' is yet another corporate metaphor by means

143

of which Paul seeks to consolidate the Church as a kind of 'true Israel', the eschatological people of God, an autonomous polity bearing witness to the kingdom of God, the lordship of Christ and the power of the Spirit.

As to what kind of alternative society the church body is to be: this is summed up in the designation of the body as 'the body *of Christ*': 'For just as the body is one and has many members, and all the members of the body, though many, are one body, so it is with Christ. For by one Spirit we were all baptized into one body – Jews or Greeks, slaves or free – and all were made to drink of one Spirit' (12.12–13). In other words, belonging by baptism to Christ in the power of the indwelling Spirit creates a new solidarity that transcends the old divisions. In this new solidarity, there is to be unity based on an acceptance of the diversity of each member's 'gifts'; a recognition that the strength of the whole depends on the full contribution of the individual parts inspired by 'the same Spirit'; a humility finding expression in special concern for the 'weaker' members; and an acknowledgement of the need for order, since 'God has appointed in the church first apostles, second prophets, third teachers ...' (12.28).[11]

Noticeable in all this is the way power indicators in the society-at-large (status, rank, birth, gender, education and occupation) are left behind or reinterpreted in relation to Christ and the Spirit. Noticeable also is the shift from competitive social relations to relations of mutual responsibility and interdependence where what is important is the 'building up' of the community (14.12, 26b). Even the restrictions on the role of women (14.33b–36; cf. 11.2–16) – controversial as they were then and doubtless contributing to the baleful tradition of Christian misogyny ever since – may be understood, first and foremost, as part of Paul's overall attempt to restrain forces threatening the disintegration of the Church: for the instructions he gives occur in the wider context of teaching about the proper ordering of worship (11.2—14.40), and represent an attempt to modify a (charismatic-gnostic) spirituality that knows no bounds in favour of a spirituality controlled by a concern with what makes for 'peace' in the fellowship (14.33a).

## *Apostolic autobiography and the nature of leadership*

In Paul's use of the metaphor of the body of Christ in 1 Corinthians, there is no reflection on who is the head. This development takes place later, in Colossians and Ephesians (Cf. Colossians 1.18; 2.19; Ephesians 1.22–3; 4.15–16; 5.23). But this does not mean that 1 Corinthians is lacking when it comes to the issue of authority and leadership in the community. In particular, Paul's appeal to his own apostolic autobiography provides significant material for reflection on the nature of Christian leadership.

Read superficially, it would be easy to interpret Paul's frequent self-reference in 1 Corinthians as highly egotistical – and, of course, those hostile to Paul commonly accuse him of being domineering and manipulative. However, this may be a way only of protecting ourselves against the things that are uncongenial in what Paul says. A closer, more historically sensitive reading leads to a different conclusion: Paul, in common with other Greco-Roman moralists of his day, presents himself as a paradigm of the behaviour he seeks to commend to his addressees. The rationale is straightforward. These moralists shared the conviction 'that example was far superior to precept and logical analysis as a means of illustrating and reinforcing appeals to pursue a particular mode of life'.[12] Paul himself puts it quite succinctly and christocentrically: 'Be imitators of me, as I am of Christ' (11.1).

There are two points in particular where Paul refers at length to his own example in order to provide a paradigm of how he wants the Corinthians – and especially those who style themselves 'the strong' – to behave. The first comes in 1 Corinthians 9, which interrupts Paul's instructions 'concerning things sacrificed to idols', in chapters 8–10. The second comes in 1 Corinthians 13, which interrupts Paul's instructions 'concerning spiritual gifts', in chapters 12–14. But understood from the perspective of epistolary instruction and the common practice of Greco-Roman moralists, 1 Corinthians 9 and 13 are not interruptions or digressions at all. Rather, each passage is integrally related to its specific context, as Paul presents his own behaviour as a practical guide for the Corinthians to follow.

So, to persuade the strong to refrain from exercising their 'authority' to eat food sacrificed to idols – thus threatening the unity of the Church by causing grave offence to the weak – Paul shifts to the first person singular to show what he himself does: 'Therefore, if food is a cause of my brother's falling, I will never eat meat, lest I cause my brother to fall' (8.13). He then proceeds to give an extended example from his own practice as their apostle of how, at considerable social and economic cost, he refrains from exercising his own 'authority' to receive financial support from the Corinthians so as not to place any hindrance in the way of their receiving the gospel (9.1–18). For Paul the apostle, true freedom is found in being able to restrict one's freedom – which means becoming like a slave – for the sake of 'saving' as many people as possible: 'For though I am free with respect to all, I have made myself a slave to all, so that I might win the more of them. ... I have become all things to all people, that I might by all means save some' (9.19–22 NRSV; cf. 10.31–3).[13] This is not an easy path, as the language of enslavement suggests. It involves putting the interests of others first: for the sake of Christ, the gospel of Christ, and the brother or sister for whom Christ died. Not surprisingly, therefore, the argument reaches a climax with yet another piece of instruction about the body: in this case, Paul's own body which, like that of an athlete, has to be disciplined and trained if the prize (consequent upon building up the body of Christ) is to be attained (9.24–7).

The second instance follows the same pattern. In the middle of instruction intended to counter the threat to church unity posed, this time, by disorder and confusion (14.33) in the exercise of the so-called 'spiritual gifts', Paul reverts to the first person singular in order once more to offer a concrete paradigm of the 'more excellent way' of love, the practice of which will make the Corinthians' worship upbuilding rather than catastrophic for the community. Carl Holladay points out that 'Commentators have long noticed Paul's use of the first person singular here [in 1 Corinthians 13], but it is ordinarily taken in a general rather than a strictly autobiographical sense.'[14] He argues convincingly, however, that it has to be taken literally. Paul is talking about himself: his own gifts governed by love (13.1–3), his own understanding of the phenomenology of love (13.4–7), and his own insight into the eschatological finality of a love already present and never-ending (13.8–13). Whereas the immaturity of the Corinthian 'strong' has caused them to regard 'knowledge' as the ultimate eschatological reality, allowing them to lord it over others, Paul presents himself as one who has 'grown up' spiritually and who can testify otherwise: not 'knowledge' but 'love' is the ultimate eschatological reality – because, as he has pointed out earlier, '"knowledge" puffs up, but love builds up' (8.1b). On this paradigmatic basis, Paul can then return in chapter 14 to the second person plural, prefacing his ongoing instructions about 'spiritual gifts' with the overriding command: 'Make love your aim' (14.1).

We need to be wary of being simplistic in trying to articulate what all this implies about Paul as a leader. Nevertheless, it seems clear that Paul did not shirk the costly role of exercising leadership and authority in the Corinthian community. It is clear also that Paul sought to lead by exemplifying in his own apostolic life the virtues and practices that he invited his fellow-believers to imitate. Finally, Paul's goal in exercising leadership was the consolidation not of his own power and status, but of the oneness and growth of the community 'in Christ'.

## Conclusion

In the light of this examination of 1 Corinthians, we may conclude with the simple observation that Paul's primary concern was not with 'community' in the abstract, but with how to respond and bear witness to the startling, new revelation of the grace of God in the cross and resurrection of Christ and the gift of the Spirit.[15] It was because this new revelation decisively burst the bounds of previous conceptions of space and time, individual and social personhood, power and authority, and life and death, that Paul and his contemporaries were obliged to think again.

To put it another way, Paul was not a sociologist before his time in trying to understand what 'community' is and why people talk about it endlessly and in so many different ways! Rather, Paul was a Jew zealous for the law, the temple, the land and the elect people of Israel, whose life was turned upside down 'through a revelation of Jesus Christ' and a commission to be apostle to the Gentiles (Galatians 1.12,16). In consequence, Paul's talk is not about 'community', but about how Jews and Gentiles, men and women, slaves and freeborn can embody and celebrate the eschatological life of the kingdom of God. This is not a matter of social engineering in quest of the 'ideal community'. It is a matter of participation in divine love in the power of the Spirit and testifying of that love and power to others.

As we have seen, this 'participation' (*koinonia*) involves a number of things. First, it involves an ongoing transformation of life in the light of Christ's cross and resurrection. Second, there is the importance of sacramental gatherings that unite those gathered in practices with water, bread and wine – 'holy things' grounded in a shared narrative of salvation. Third, it involves a holy and disciplined lifestyle embodied in every aspect of people's social relations and expressing their new identity as 'the body of Christ'. Finally, it requires the acceptance of leadership exercised by those whose depth of spiritual maturity is shown by their renunciation of 'boasting' in favour of that 'more excellent way' of love. These are principles and practices for the common good: the common good of the Church and of society as a whole.

# Conclusion:

# A P(olitically) C(orrect) Bible?

In an article in the *Church Times* of 15 September 1995, entitled 'Editor defends PC Bible', the paper's American correspondent reported on the response to the publication by Oxford University Press in the United States of a new version of the Bible called *The New Testament and Psalms: A New Inclusive Translation*. According to the correspondent, Gustav Spohn:

> Fierce criticism has greeted the American publication of an inclusive-language version of the New Testament and Psalms. ... Because it removes much language deemed sexist or racist in the liberal theological camp, it has been assailed by conservatives as attempting to be politically correct at the expense of theological and linguistic integrity. The conservative *Christianity Today*, for example, said in an editorial printed in February, 'We must never censor God's words, scissoring our way through scripture like Thomas Jefferson did, when he attempted to winnow out the miraculous and preserve only the ethical teaching of the New Testament. Censorship is exactly what the scholars who produced the "New Inclusive Translation" have indulged in. May their work gather dust in America's bookstores.' More recently, on 5 September, the *Wall Street Journal* ran an editorial that began, 'We suppose it had to happen. Sooner or later someone was bound to notice that the Word of God isn't politically correct.'

There is a serious issue here. In another form, we have met it already in the complaints of Sir Ian McKellen and Mrs Anne Spicer. For them, the Bible so offends modern sensibilities that it ought to be censored or even banned outright. For the 'conservatives' cited above, however, it is precisely because the Bible offends modern sensibilities that it still speaks as the 'Word of God'! In the light of the ground we have covered in the preceding chapters, what might we want to say both to the editors of the new 'PC Bible' and to their critics?

First, in so far as political correctness is a shorthand for a society's concern to treat its members fairly and to combat prejudice on grounds of gender, race or disability in a society that is liberal, pluralistic and multicultural,[1] the use of inclusive language can be a useful corrective, thoroughly in keeping with the biblical vision of the love of God for all humankind, especially the poor and the victimized. So if inclusive language makes visible those whom prejudice renders invisible or brings into the centre those whom unjust social structures have marginalized, it is performing an important Christian service. It may be the case that some who criticize political correctness in Bible translations or in liturgical revision fail sufficiently to recognize the potential of these modifications in language for achieving the goal of building a more egalitarian society.

A second point worth making is that a PC Bible may be an attempt, however fragile and fallible, to allow the Bible to speak in ways that men and women today can understand. As with Rudolf Bultmann's programme of demythologization a generation or more ago, it can be seen as reflecting a Christian concern to challenge people with the *true* 'scandal' of Christianity, instead of placing unnecessary obstacles of language and worldview in their way. As one of the editors of the New Inclusive Translation is quoted as saying: 'Because of the role it plays in the Church, every generation must render the Bible in its own idiom; and because of recent, increased sensitivity to the many ways in which our language has put down various peoples, it became imperative to provide people with a version of the scriptures that reflected the change in sensitivity.'[2]

It may also reflect a quite proper recognition that theological discrimination and appropriation is required in interpreting the Bible. What is important for Christian faith is not some kind of 'mechanical' belief in the words of the text *per se*, but an acceptance grounded in the experience of Christians down the ages that the words of the text constitute a trustworthy testimony to the divine Trinity to whom we belong in worship and service. In practice, this means that not every word of Scripture is of equal significance for every generation of readers, that some parts have to be (re)interpreted in the light of other parts, and that the Scriptures are not an end in themselves but have their proper place in the ongoing life of the Church as it seeks to know and do God's will under the guidance of the Holy Spirit. May it not be the case that an inclusive-language, PC Bible has a part to play in that process?

But there is another side to all this, and there are equally serious reasons for doubting the wisdom of the PC Bible, however well intentioned its editors. The main concern has to do with the wisdom of constantly 'adjusting' the text of the Bible to make it conform to what each new generation regards as 'acceptable'. The first danger here is that the text of the Bible becomes relatively unstable. As a result, it not only becomes difficult to memorize, with the consequent impoverishment of Christian spirituality, but it also becomes difficult to build liturgical worship around, since the firm foundations provided by the words and imagery of the text are constantly being undermined. This is a serious issue if what has been said in earlier chapters is true – namely, that the Bible is the book of the Church and helps to constitute the identity of the Church by its central place in worship and in spiritual formation.

Another danger is that the Bible may be at risk of trivialization. Instead of serving as a beacon of truth and a witness to a God who is transcendent, it is liable to become little more than a cultural icon of considerable plasticity, able to be moulded and remoulded according to prevailing tastes and values.[3] To repeat the point made in Chapter 2, it is not just we who interpret the Bible (in terms of our growing understanding of the truth of God and the gospel of Christ): it is also the case that the Bible, as 'revelation', stands over against, and interprets, us.

Related to this is another theological point: that, ironically, the PC Bible fails to take the problem of 'political incorrectness' in the Bible seriously enough. It is superficial, and only papers over the cracks. Changing a word here and there may be little more than a distraction from the *real* issue of 'political incorrectness' that is often overlooked: that the God to whom the Bible testifies is a God notorious for his refusal to conform to the prevailing norms of correctness of any society in any age!

By this I mean not that God is malign or unpredictable or perverse, so that he never measures up to human standards of right and wrong. On the contrary, what I mean is that God's love is so bountiful, his fidelity so constant, and his justice so true that any notion of 'political correctness' is quite incapable of providing a satisfactory measure! God is 'politically incorrect' on a massive scale. That is to say, he refuses to be *brought down* to the level of what the so-called liberal West (or whatever kind of society) accepts as 'correct'. The God who chooses Israel to be a 'light to the nations' and who becomes incarnate in Jesus of Nazareth and suffers death on a cross for the redemption of a creation in bondage to sin is a God who shows that political correctness is *too small an idea* to do justice to the mystery of divine grace.

Political correctness may well have its place as a way of guarding the rights of minorities in a pluralistic society. However, from a Christian theological point of view, the rights of minorities are guarded best when people in Church and society practise conformity to a higher moral vision altogether: that love of God and of neighbour to which the Bible in both its Testaments, and with all its awkward 'problem texts', bears unique testimony. That is why we do well to accept the Church's invitation to the Bible: not because the Bible is politically correct, but because it bears witness to the triune God in whose image, and with the prejudice of love alone, we are all made.

# Notes

## Preface

1 See Nicola Slee, ed., *Testimony to Transformation: a celebration of the Aston Training Scheme in its 18th year* (Birmingham, Aston Training Scheme, 1995); also, Norman Todd, *A Thing Called Aston. An Experiment in Reflective Learning* (London, Church House Publishing, 1987).

## 1  Hate-mail Or Love-letter?

1 See further, Stephen E. Fowl and L. Gregory Jones, *Reading in Communion. Scripture and Ethics in Christian Life* (London, SPCK, 1991).

2 See Gordon W. Lathrop, *Holy Things. A Liturgical Theology* (Minneapolis, Fortress Press, 1993).

3 See further, Daniel Migliore, *Faith Seeking Understanding* (Grand Rapids, Eerdmans, 1991), ch. 3.

4 See further, Charles M. Wood, *The Formation of Christian Understanding* (Philadelphia, Westminster Press, 1981).

5 See, for example, the collection of essays edited by Carl E. Braaten and Robert W. Jenson, *Reclaiming the Bible for the Church* (Grand Rapids, Eerdmans, 1995).

6 Discussed further in two books by James Barr, *Fundamentalism* (London, SCM, 1977) and *Escaping from Fundamentalism* (London, SCM, 1984). See also Kathleen C. Boone, *The Bible Tells Them So. The Discourse of Protestant Fundamentalism* (London, SCM, 1990).

## 2  The Art of Interpretation

1 See further, Robert Morgan with John Barton, *Biblical Interpretation* (Oxford, Oxford University Press, 1988), esp. ch. 8.

2 See also on this point the comments of the great Orthodox theologian Georges Florovsky, in his *Bible, Church, Tradition: An Eastern Orthodox View* (Belmont, MA, Nordland, 1972), ch. 1, 'The Lost Scriptural Mind'.

3 As well as Morgan with Barton, *Biblical Interpretation*, ch. 7, see, more recently, the relevant essays in Joel B. Green, ed., *Hearing the New Testament. Strategies for Interpretation* (Grand Rapids, Eerdmans, 1995).

4 See further, L. William Countryman, *Dirt, Greed and Sex. Sexual Ethics in the New*

*Testament and their Implications for Today* (London, SCM, 1989).

5 Daniel Migliore, *Faith Seeking Understanding* (Grand Rapids, Eerdmans, 1991), p. 54.

6 See Charles E. Reagan and David Stewart, eds, *Paul Ricoeur. An Anthology of his Work* (Boston, Beacon Press, 1978), esp. part V.

7 See further, Christopher Rowland and Mark Corner, *Liberating Exegesis. The Challenge of Liberation Theology to Biblical Studies* (London, SPCK, 1990).

8 See Karl Barth's 1921 Preface to the Second Edition of his ground-breaking work, *The Epistle to the Romans* (London, Oxford University Press, 1933), pp. 2–15. Cf. Peter Selby, 'Who Is Really in Charge? – Bible or Church?', in John V. Taylor *et al.*, *Bishops on the Bible* (London, Triangle/SPCK, 1993), pp. 32–52, at pp. 43–4:

> For all that I have said about the dialectical way in which the Bible has to be interpreted in relation to our experience as individuals and as the Church, I also have to say that I have seen too often what happens when churches fail to root themselves securely enough in the biblical experience. When I have seen the preaching in so-called liberal churches turn into mere chat without any leverage on the life of congregation or members ... or when Anglo-Catholicism turns into an esoteric and self-indulgent enterprise for the maintaining of customs and practices long after they have ceased to nourish, then mostly it is that the essential dialogue with Scripture has ceased to play its proper part in the life of the community.

## 3  Two Testaments, One Bible

1 *The Common Bible* (New York and Glasgow, Collins, 1971 edn).

2 See, for example, James D. Smart, *The Strange Silence of the Bible in the Church* (London, SCM, 1970), pp. 19ff.

3 See further, Harry Y. Gamble, *The New Testament Canon. Its Making and Meaning* (Philadelphia, Fortress Press, 1985), ch. III; also, James L. Kugel and Rowan A. Greer, *Early Biblical Interpretation* (Philadelphia, Westminster Press, 1986), esp. pp. 109–25.

4 Superb on this is the work of the Jewish scholar Jon D. Levenson, *The Hebrew Bible, the Old Testament, and Historical Criticism* (Louisville, Westminster/John Knox Press, 1993). On the Christian side, the work of Brevard S. Childs, amongst others, has been of crucial importance. He summarizes his position in his recent essay, 'On Reclaiming the Bible for Christian Theology', in Carl E. Braaten and Robert W. Jenson, eds, *Reclaiming the Bible for the Church*, (Grand Rapids, Eerdmans, 1995), pp. 1–17.

5 For a brief but valuable account, see George M. Marsden, *Understanding Fundamentalism and Evangelicalism* (Grand Rapids, Eerdmans, 1991), chs 5–6.

6 For one trenchant account, see Thomas C. Oden, *After Modernity ... What?* (Grand Rapids, Zondervan, 1990), Part One.

7 The issues are discussed by Walter Moberly in his essay, '"Old Testament" and

NOTES

"New Testament": The Propriety of the Terms for Christian Theology', *Theology*, vol. XCV (1992), pp. 26–32.

8 One way into this question – not explored here, but none the less very important – is to attend to the ways in which the Hebrew Bible is important for Jews. As well as the work of Jon D. Levenson, cited in note 4, I have found two authors especially helpful: Rabbi Jonathan Magonet, in *A Rabbi's Bible* (London, SCM, 1991), and Chaim Potok, in novels such as *The Chosen* and *The Promise*.

9 See further, Kugel and Greer, *Early Biblical Interpretation*, pp. 126–54.

10 See further, James D. G. Dunn, *Christology in the Making* (London, SCM, 1980); and, most recently, John Barclay and John Sweet, eds, *Early Christian Thought in its Jewish Context* (Cambridge, Cambridge University Press, 1996).

11 This is well brought out in Trevor Dennis's book, *Lo and Behold! The Power of Old Testament Storytelling* (London, SPCK, 1991); and also in the many works of Walter Brueggemann – such as *The Prophetic Imagination* (London, SCM, 1992), and *Hopeful Imagination. Prophetic Voices in Exile* (London, SCM, 1992).

12 See further, Terence E. Fretheim, *The Suffering of God* (Philadelphia, Fortress Press, 1984).

13 See, on this, Andrew Louth's marvellous book *Discerning the Mystery. An Essay on the Nature of Theology* (Oxford, Clarendon Press, 1983).

14 See Brevard S. Childs, *Old Testament Theology in a Canonical Context* (London, SCM, 1985).

15 David L. Baker, *Two Testaments, One Bible. A Study of the Theological Relationship Between the Old and New Testaments* (Leicester, Apollos, 1991, 2nd edn).

16 See Baker, *Two Testaments, One Bible*, ch. 3.

17 See Baker, *Two Testaments, One Bible*, ch. 4.

18 See further, Walter Moberly, *The Old Testament of the Old Testament* (Minneapolis, Fortress Press, 1992), esp. ch. 5.

19 See Baker, *Two Testaments, One Bible*, ch. 5.

20 See Baker, *Two Testaments, One Bible*, ch. 6.

21 See, most recently, Robert Morgan's essay, 'On the Unity of Scripture', in Jon Davies *et al.*, eds, *Words Remembered, Texts Renewed* (Sheffield, Sheffield Academic Press, 1995), pp. 395–413.

# 4   The Medium Is The Message?

1 See further the essays in Garrett Green, ed., *Scriptural Authority and Narrative Interpretation* (Philadelphia, Fortress Press, 1987); also, Charles M. Wood, *The Formation of Christian Understanding*, esp. pp. 100–1.

2 See, especially, David J. A. Clines, *The Theme of the Pentateuch* (Sheffield, JSOT Press, 1984); also, Michael Fishbane, *Text and Texture. Close Readings of Selected Biblical Texts* (New York, Schocken Books, 1979), pp. 3–16; and Trevor J. Dennis, *Lo and Behold! The Power of Old Testament Storytelling* (London, SPCK, 1991), ch. 1.

3 Very useful is Walter Moberly, 'Did The Serpent Get It Right?', *Journal of Theological Studies*, NS, vol. 39 (1988), pp. 1–27.

155

4 See on this, Jouette Bassler, 'Adam, Eve, and the Pastor. The Use of Genesis 2—3 in the Pastoral Epistles', in G. A. Robbins, ed., *Genesis 1—3 in the History of Exegesis* (Lewiston, Edwin Mellen Press, 1988), pp. 43–65.

5 See, in general, Brevard S. Childs, *Old Testament Theology in a Canonical Context* (London, SCM, 1985), chs 5–8.

6 See further, Jacob Neusner, *Torah Through the Ages* (London, SCM, 1990); also, at a more popular level, Lionel Blue, *To Heaven with Scribes and Pharisees* (London, Darton, Longman and Todd, 1975).

7 For historical essays, see D. A. Carson, ed., *From Sabbath to Lord's Day* (Grand Rapids, Zondervan, 1982); and, in recent systematic theology, see Jürgen Moltmann, *God in Creation* (London, SCM, 1985), ch. XI.

8 See Daniel Migliore, *Faith Seeking Understanding* (Grand Rapids, Eerdmans, 1991), p. 47.

## 5   Why Four Gospels?

1 For an excellent consideration of this dimension of the Christian canon, see further, Robert Morgan, 'The Hermeneutical Significance of Four Gospels', in J. L. Mays, ed., *Interpreting the Gospels* (Philadelphia, Fortress Press, 1981), pp. 41–54. Also relevant is Brevard S. Childs, *The New Testament as Canon: An Introduction* (London, SCM, 1984), chs 9 and 10.

2 A useful introduction to these issues is James D. G. Dunn, *The Evidence for Jesus* (London, SCM, 1985). More demanding is N. T. Wright, *The New Testament and the People of God* (London, SPCK, 1992), parts I and II.

3 See further, Sandra M. Schneiders, *The Revelatory Text. Interpreting the New Testament as Sacred Scripture* (San Francisco, HarperCollins, 1991).

4 See in general, David M. Stanley, *Jesus in Gethsemane* (New York, Paulist Press, 1980); also, Brian E. Beck, 'Gethsemane in the Four Gospels', *Epworth Review*, vol. 15 (1988), pp. 57–65. Most recent is Raymond E. Brown's massive work, *The Death of the Messiah, Vol. I* (New York, Doubleday, 1994), at pp. 110–234.

5 See further, Richard Burridge, *What are the Gospels? A Comparison with Graeco-Roman Biography* (Cambridge, Cambridge University Press, 1992).

6 On prayer in Mark, see Susan E. Dowd, *Prayer, Power, and the Problem of Suffering: Mark 11:22–25 in the Context of Markan Theology* (Atlanta, Scholars Press, 1988).

7 See further, Joel B. Green, 'Jesus on the Mount of Olives (Luke 22.39–46)', *Journal for the Study of the New Testament*, vol. 26 (1986), pp. 29–48.

8 On the significance of prayer in Luke, see further, Stephen C. Barton, *The Spirituality of the Gospels* (London, SPCK, 1992), esp. pp. 87–91.

9 On prayer in the Johannine literature, see further, Marianne Meye Thompson, 'Intercession in the Johannine Community: 1 John 5.16 in the Context of the Gospel and Epistles of John', in M. J. Wilkins and T. Paige, eds, *Worship, Theology and Ministry in the Early Church* (Sheffield, JSOT Press, 1992), pp. 225–45.

## 6 Did It Happen And Does It Matter?

1 Compare on this, Robert Morgan's essay, 'Can the Critical Study of Scripture Provide a Doctrinal Norm?', *Journal of Religion*, vol. 76 (1996), pp. 206–32, esp. pp. 217 ff. on 'John at the Center of New Testament Theology'.

2 See further, Robert Morgan with John Barton, *Biblical Interpretation* (Oxford, Oxford University Press, 1988), ch. 6.

3 For an expert survey, see D. Moody Smith, *The Theology of the Gospel of John* (Cambridge, Cambridge University Press, 1995).

4 See further, Robert Morgan, 'Faith', in *idem*, ed., *The Religion of the Incarnation* (Bristol, Bristol Classical Press, 1989), pp. 1–32.

5 C. H. Dodd, *Historical Tradition and the Fourth Gospel* (Cambridge, Cambridge University Press, 1963).

6 Nicholas Lash, *Theology on the Way to Emmaus* (London, SCM, 1986), p. 25.

## 7 What About 'Problem Texts'?

1 See, for example, Mary J. Evans, *Woman in the Bible* (Exeter, Paternoster Press, 1983), and John R. W. Stott, *Issues Facing Christians Today* (London, Marshall, Morgan and Scott, 1984), pp. 234–57.

2 This stance is particularly clear in Daphne Hampson, *Theology and Feminism* (Oxford, Basil Blackwell, 1990), ch. 3.

3 See, for example, Mary Hayter, *The New Eve in Christ. The Use and Abuse of the Bible in the Debate About Women in the Church* (London, SPCK, 1987); also, John Barton, *What Is the Bible?* (London, Triangle/SPCK, 1991), ch. 8, 'Is the Bible Sexist?'.

4 See, further, the brilliant essay by Nicholas Lash, 'What Might Martyrdom Mean?', in his collection of essays, *Theology on the Way to Emmaus* (London, SCM, 1986), ch. 6.

5 See, most recently, Frances Young, *The Art of Performance* (London, Darton, Longman and Todd, 1990).

6 As shown, for example, in the recent survey by the Roman Catholic theologian Joseph A. Fitzmyer, '*Kephalē* in I Corinthians 11:3', *Interpretation*, vol. 47 (1993), pp. 52–9.

7 Examples of this strategy are: Krister Stendahl, *The Bible and the Role of Women* (Philadelphia, Fortress Press, 1966); Robin Scroggs, 'Paul and the Eschatological Woman', *Journal of the American Academy of Religion*, vol. 40 (1972), pp. 283–303; Elisabeth Schüssler Fiorenza, *In Memory of Her. A Feminist Theological Reconstruction of Christian Origins* (London, SCM, 1983).

8 See, further, the provocative essay by David C. Steinmetz, 'The Superiority of Pre-Critical Exegesis', *Ex Auditu*, vol. 1 (1985), pp. 74–82, originally published in *Theology Today*, vol. 37 (1980), pp. 27–38.

9 For several examples, see the essays collected in Ann Loades's book, *Feminist Theology. A Reader* (London, SCM, 1990), Part One.

10 On which, see, for example, James D. G. Dunn, *The Living Word* (London, SCM, 1987), pp. 3–24, and most recently, his essay, 'Historical Text as Historical Text:

Some Basic Hermeneutical Reflections in Relation to the New Testament', in Jon Davies *et al.*, eds, *Words Remembered, Texts Renewed* (Sheffield, Sheffield Academic Press, 1995), pp. 340–59.

11 Robert Morgan, 'Feminist Theological Interpretation of the New Testament', in Janet M. Soskice, ed., *After Eve. Women, Theology and the Christian Tradition* (London, Marshall Pickering, 1990), p. 26.

12 On the metaphor of performance as a fruitful way to understand the art of biblical interpretation, see especially Lash, *Theology on the Way to Emmaus*, pp. 37–46, 75–92, discussed further below, in Chapter 8.

13 See also, Stephen C. Barton, 'Women, Jesus and the Gospels', in Richard Holloway, ed., *Who Needs Feminism? Men Respond to Feminism in the Church* (London, SPCK, 1991), pp. 32–58.

14 See Rudolf Bultmann, 'New Testament and Mythology', in Hans-Werner Bartsch, ed., *Kerygma and Myth. A Theological Debate* (London, SPCK, 1972), pp. 1–44.

15 See, further, the other essays in Bartsch, ed., *Kerygma and Myth*; also, Anthony C. Thiselton, *The Two Horizons. New Testament Hermeneutics and Philosophical Description* (Grand Rapids, Eerdmans, 1980), chs VIII–X.

16 See, further, the useful survey by Werner Jeanrond, *Theological Hermeneutics. Development and Significance* (London, SCM, 1994).

# 8 How Then Shall we Live?

1 In passing, it is worth drawing attention to a striking innovation in biblical interpretation, known as 'bibliodrama', which builds on this perception. Working on the assumption that the biblical texts were written in the first instance to be read aloud to an audience of listeners, bibliodrama seeks to rediscover their transformative dynamic by means of dramatic rendition. The British actor Alec McCowen, for example, has become well known for his stage performances of the King James Version of the Gospel of Mark. Also, the Swiss theologian Walter Hollenweger has been at the forefront of attempts to engage a wide variety of people with the power of biblical narrative through bibliodrama. What is noticeable in this kind of approach is the dual contribution of performer(s) and audience to the discovery of meaning in the biblical text, something that the more strictly historical approach to interpretation often neglects. See also Björn Krondorfer, ed., *Body and Bible. Interpreting and Experiencing Biblical Narratives* (Philadelphia, Trinity Press International, 1992).

2 Among other writers I have discovered who use the analogy (in a variety of ways) are Stephen E. Fowl and L. Gregory Jones, *Reading in Communion. Scripture and Ethics in Christian Life* (London, SPCK, 1991), especially ch. 6; Mary McClintock Fulkerson, *Changing the Subject. Women's Discourses and Feminist Theology* (Minneapolis, Fortress Press, 1994), especially chs. 3–5; Kevin J. Vanhoozer, 'The World Well Staged? Theology, Culture, and Hermeneutics', in D. A. Carson and J. D. Woodbridge, eds, *God and Culture. Essays in Honor of Carl F. Henry* (Grand Rapids, Eerdmans, 1993), pp. 1–30; Rowan Williams, 'The Literal

Sense of Scripture', *Modern Theology*, vol. 7 (1991), pp. 121–34; and N. T. Wright, 'How Can the Bible Be Authoritative?' (the Laing Lecture 1989 and the Griffith Thomas Lecture 1989; unpublished MS), pp. 11f., 17–18.
3 It is reprinted in his book, *Theology on the Way to Emmaus* (London, SCM, 1986), pp. 37-46.
4 Lash, *Theology on the Way to Emmaus*, p. 40.
5 Peter Brook, *The Empty Space* (Harmondsworth, Penguin Books, 1972), pp. 11–46.
6 See, further, the essays in R. S. Sugirtharajah, ed., *Voices from the Margin. Interpreting the Bible in the Third World* (London, SPCK, 1991).
7 Lash, *Theology on the Way to Emmaus*, p. 43.
8 Important in this respect is the final chapter of Fowl and Jones, *Reading in Communion*, on 'Living and Dying in the Word: Dietrich Bonhoeffer as Performer of Scripture'.
9 See, further, Jeffrey B. Gibson, *The Temptations of Jesus in Early Christianity* (Sheffield, JSOT, 1995); also, Austin Farrer, *The Triple Victory. Christ's Temptation according to St Matthew* (Cambridge MA, Cowley, 1990).

## 9   *The Bible For The Common Good*

1 Cf. Fred B. Craddock, 'Preaching to Corinthians', *Interpretation*, vol. XLIV (1990), pp. 158–68.
2 Jonathan Sacks, *The Persistence of Faith. Religion, Morality and Society in a Secular Age* (London, Weidenfeld and Nicolson, 1991), especially pp. 84–94. Cf. also his *Faith in the Future* (London, Darton, Longman and Todd, 1995), pp. 55–8.
3 See, further, Margaret M. Mitchell, *Paul and the Rhetoric of Reconciliation* (Louisville, Westminster/John Knox Press, 1993).
4 See, in general, Gerd Theissen, *The Social Setting of Pauline Christianity* (Edinburgh, T. & T. Clark, 1982), pp. 145–74.
5 On the idea of memory as helping to constitute a community, see Stanley Hauerwas, *A Community of Character* (Notre Dame, University of Notre Dame Press, 1981), pp. 53–71.
6 See, in general, Craig Dykstra's excellent essay, 'Disciplines: Repentance, Prayer and Service', in R. P. Hamel and K. R. Hines, eds, *Introduction to Christian Ethics. A Reader* (New York, Paulist Press, 1989), pp. 293–307.
7 See, further, Wayne A. Meeks, '"Since then you would need to go out of the world": Group Boundaries in Pauline Christianity', in T. J. Ryan, ed., *Critical History and Biblical Faith: New Testament Perspectives* (Billanova, Pa., College Theology Society, 1979), pp. 1–23.
8 See, most recently, Dale B. Martin, *The Corinthian Body* (New Haven and London, Yale University Press, 1995); also, Wayne A. Meeks, *The Origins of Christian Morality* (New Haven and London, Yale University Press, 1993), pp. 130–49.
9 Mary Douglas, *Natural Symbols* (London, Barrie and Jenkins, 1973, 2nd edn), p. 98.

# NOTES

10 See, further, Mitchell, *Paul and the Rhetoric of Reconciliation*, pp. 157–64.

11 See, further, James D. G. Dunn, *Jesus and the Spirit* (London, SCM, 1975), chs. VIII–IX; idem, *1 Corinthians* (Sheffield, Sheffield Academic Press, 1995), ch. 5.

12 Carl R. Holladay, '1 Corinthians 13. Paul as Apostolic Paradigm', in D. L. Balch *et al.*, eds, *Greeks, Romans and Christians* (Philadelphia, Fortress Press, 1990), pp. 80–98, at p. 84.

13 See further on this, Stephen C. Barton, '"All Things to All People": Paul and the Law in the Light of 1 Corinthians 9.19–23', in James D. G. Dunn, ed., *Paul and the Law* (Tübingen, Mohr/Siebeck, 1996), pp. 271–86.

14 Holladay, '1 Corinthians 13. Paul as Apostolic Paradigm', p. 88.

15 For an argument along similar lines but in relation to 1 Peter, see the excellent essay by Miroslav Wolf, 'Soft Difference. Theological Reflections on the Relation Between Church and Culture in 1 Peter', *Ex Auditu*, vol. 10 (1994), pp. 15–30. Cf. also Stanley Hauerwas, 'What Could It Mean for the Church to be Christ's Body?', *Scottish Journal of Theology*, vol. 48 (1995), pp. 1–21, at 11–15.

## Conclusion: A P(olitically) C(orrect) Bible?

1 For a useful survey article, see John Wilson, 'Political Correctness', in Paul B. Clarke and Andrew Linzey, eds, *Dictionary of Ethics, Theology and Society* (London and New York, Routledge, 1996), pp. 651–4. Relevant also is Robert Hughes, *Culture of Complaint* (London, Harvill, 1994).

2 *Church Times*, 15 September 1995, p. 2.

3 See on this, Stanley Hauerwas, *Unleashing the Scripture. Freeing the Bible from Captivity to America* (Nashville, Abingdon, 1993), especially Part One.

# Bibliography

David L. Baker, *Two Testaments, One Bible. A Study of the Theological Relationship Between the Old and New Testaments* (Leicester, Apollos, 1991, 2nd edn).

John Barclay and John Sweet, eds, *Early Christian Thought in its Jewish Context* (Cambridge, Cambridge University Press, 1996).

James Barr, *Fundamentalism* (London, SCM, 1977).

James Barr, *Escaping from Fundamentalism* (London, SCM, 1984).

John Barton, *What Is the Bible?* (London, Triangle/SPCK, 1991).

Stephen C. Barton, 'Women, Jesus and the Gospels', in Richard Holloway, ed., *Who Needs Feminism? Men Respond to Feminism in the Church* (London, SPCK, 1991), pp. 32–58.

Stephen C. Barton, *The Spirituality of the Gospels* (London, SPCK, 1992).

Stephen C. Barton, '"All Things to All People": Paul and the Law in the Light of 1 Corinthians 9.19–23', in James D. G. Dunn, ed., *Paul and the Law* (Tübingen, Mohr/Siebeck, 1996), pp. 271–86.

Jouette Bassler, 'Adam, Eve, and the Pastor. The Use of Genesis 2—3 in the Pastoral Epistles', in G. A. Robbins, ed., *Genesis 1—3 in the History of Exegesis* (Lewiston, Edwin Mellen Press, 1988), pp. 43–65.

Brian E. Beck, 'Gethsemane in the Four Gospels', *Epworth Review*, vol. 15 (1988), pp. 57–65.

Lionel Blue, *To Heaven with Scribes and Pharisees* (London, Darton, Longman and Todd, 1975).

Dietrich Bonhoeffer, *Meditating on the Word* (Cambridge, MA, Cowley, 1986).

Kathleen C. Boone, *The Bible Tells Them So. The Discourse of Protestant Fundamentalism* (London, SCM, 1990).

John Bowker, *A Year to Live* (London, SPCK, 1991).

Carl E. Braaten and Robert W. Jenson, eds, *Reclaiming the Bible for the Church* (Grand Rapids, Eerdmans, 1995).

Peter Brook, *The Empty Space* (Harmondsworth, Penguin Books, 1972).

Raymond E. Brown, *The Death of the Messiah*, 2 vols (New York, Doubleday, 1994).

Walter Brueggemann, *The Prophetic Imagination* (London, SCM, 1992).

Walter Brueggemann, *Hopeful Imagination. Prophetic Voices in Exile* (London, SCM, 1992).

Rudolf Bultmann, 'New Testament and Mythology', in Hans-Werner Bartsch, ed., *Kerygma and Myth. A Theological Debate* (London, SPCK, 1972), pp. 1–44.

# BIBLIOGRAPHY

Richard Burridge, *What Are the Gospels? A Comparison with Graeco-Roman Biography* (Cambridge, Cambridge University Press, 1992).

D. A. Carson, ed., *From Sabbath to Lord's Day* (Grand Rapids, Zondervan, 1982).

Brevard S. Childs, *The New Testament as Canon: An Introduction* (London, SCM, 1984).

Brevard S. Childs, *Old Testament Theology in a Canonical Context* (London, SCM, 1985).

Brevard S. Childs, 'On Reclaiming the Bible for Christian Theology', in Carl E. Braaten and Robert W. Jenson, eds, *Reclaiming the Bible for the Church* (Grand Rapids, Eerdmans, 1995), pp. 1–17.

David J. A. Clines, *The Theme of the Pentateuch* (Sheffield, JSOT Press, 1984).

L. William Countryman, *Dirt, Greed and Sex. Sexual Ethics in the New Testament and their Implications for Today* (London, SCM, 1989).

Fred B. Craddock, 'Preaching to Corinthians', *Interpretation*, vol. XLIV (1990), pp. 158–68.

Trevor Dennis, *Lo and Behold! The Power of Old Testament Storytelling* (London, SPCK, 1991).

C. H. Dodd, *Historical Tradition and the Fourth Gospel* (Cambridge, Cambridge University Press, 1963).

Mary Douglas, *Natural Symbols* (London, Barrie and Jenkins, 1973, 2nd edn).

Susan E. Dowd, *Prayer, Power, and the Problem of Suffering: Mark 11:22–25 in the Context of Markan Theology* (Atlanta, Scholars Press, 1988).

James D. G. Dunn, *Jesus and the Spirit* (London, SCM, 1975).

James D. G. Dunn, *Christology in the Making* (London, SCM, 1980).

James D. G. Dunn, *The Evidence for Jesus* (London, SCM, 1985).

James D. G. Dunn, *1 Corinthians* (Sheffield, Sheffield Academic Press, 1995).

James D. G. Dunn, 'Historical Text as Historical Text: Some Basic Hermeneutical Reflections in Relation to the New Testament', in Jon Davies *et al.*, eds, *Words Remembered, Texts Renewed* (Sheffield, Sheffield Academic Press, 1995), pp. 340–59.

Craig Dykstra, 'Disciplines: Repentance, Prayer and Service', in R. P. Hamel and K. R. Hines, eds, *Introduction to Christian Ethics. A Reader* (New York, Paulist Press, 1989), pp. 293–307.

Mary J. Evans, *Woman in the Bible* (Exeter, Paternoster Press, 1983).

Austin Farrer, *The Triple Victory. Christ's Temptation according to St Matthew* (Cambridge MA, Cowley, 1990).

Elisabeth Schüssler Fiorenza, *In Memory of Her. A Feminist Theological Reconstruction of Christian Origins* (London, SCM Press, 1983).

Michael Fishbane, *Text and Texture. Close Readings of Selected Biblical Texts* (New York, Schocken Books, 1979).

Joseph A. Fitzmyer, '*Kephalē* in I Corinthians 11:3', *Interpretation*, vol. 47 (1993), pp. 52–9.

# BIBLIOGRAPHY

Georges Florovsky, *Bible, Church, Tradition: An Eastern Orthodox View* (Belmont, MA, Nordland, 1972).

Stephen E. Fowl and L. Gregory Jones, *Reading in Communion. Scripture and Ethics in Christian Life* (London, SPCK, 1991).

Terence E. Fretheim, *The Suffering of God* (Philadelphia, Fortress Press, 1984).

Mary McClintock Fulkerson, *Changing the Subject. Women's Discourses and Feminist Theology* (Minneapolis, Fortress Press, 1994).

Harry Y. Gamble, *The New Testament Canon. Its Making and Meaning* (Philadelphia, Fortress Press, 1985).

Jeffrey B. Gibson, *The Temptations of Jesus in Early Christianity* (Sheffield, JSOT, 1995).

Philip Goodrich, 'The Liturgical Use of Scripture', in John V. Taylor, *et al.*, *Bishops on the Bible* (London, Triangle/SPCK, 1993), pp. 89–101.

Garrett Green, ed., *Scriptural Authority and Narrative Interpretation* (Philadelphia, Fortress Press, 1987).

Joel B. Green, 'Jesus on the Mount of Olives (Luke 22.39–46)', *Journal for the Study of the New Testament*, vol. 26 (1986), pp. 29–48.

Joel B. Green, ed., *Hearing the New Testament. Strategies for Interpretation* (Grand Rapids, Eerdmans, 1995).

Daphne Hampson, *Theology and Feminism* (Oxford, Basil Blackwell, 1990).

Dan Hardy and David Ford, *Jubilate. Theology in Praise* (London, Darton, Longman and Todd, 1984).

Stanley Hauerwas, *A Community of Character* (Notre Dame, University of Notre Dame Press, 1981).

Stanley Hauerwas, *After Christendom?* (Nashville, Abingdon Press, 1991).

Stanley Hauerwas, *Unleashing the Scripture. Freeing the Bible from Captivity to America* (Nashville, Abingdon, 1993).

Stanley Hauerwas, 'What Could it Mean for the Church to be Christ's Body?', *Scottish Journal of Theology*, vol. 48 (1995), pp.1–21.

Mary Hayter, *The New Eve in Christ. The Use and Abuse of the Bible in the Debate about Women in the Church* (London, SPCK, 1987).

Abraham Heschel, *The Sabbath: Its Meaning for Modern Man* (New York, Noonday Press, 1990).

Carl R. Holladay, '1 Corinthians 13. Paul as Apostolic Paradigm', in D. L. Balch *et al.*, eds, *Greeks, Romans and Christians* (Philadelphia, Fortress Press, 1990), pp. 80–98.

David Hope, 'Prayer and the Scriptures', in John V. Taylor *et al.*, *Bishops on the Bible* (London, Triangle/SPCK, 1993), pp. 68–88.

Robert Hughes, *Culture of Complaint* (London, Harvill, 1994).

Werner Jeanrond, *Theological Hermeneutics. Development and Significance* (London, SCM, 1994).

Björn Krondorfer, ed., *Body and Bible. Interpreting and Experiencing Biblical*

# BIBLIOGRAPHY

*Narratives* (Philadelphia, Trinity Press International, 1992).

James L. Kugel and Rowan A. Greer, *Early Biblical Interpretation* (Philadelphia, Westminster Press, 1986).

Nicholas Lash, *Theology on the Way to Emmaus* (London, SCM, 1986).

Gordon W. Lathrop, *Holy Things. A Liturgical Theology* (Minneapolis, Fortress Press, 1993).

Jon D. Levenson, *The Hebrew Bible, the Old Testament, and Historical Criticism* (Louisville, Westminster/John Knox Press, 1993).

Ann Loades, ed., *Feminist Theology. A Reader* (London, SPCK, 1990).

Andrew Louth, *Discerning the Mystery. An Essay on the Nature of Theology* (Oxford, Clarendon Press, 1983).

Jonathan Magonet, *A Rabbi's Bible* (London, SCM, 1991).

George M. Marsden, *Understanding Fundamentalism and Evangelicalism* (Grand Rapids, Eerdmans, 1991).

Dale B. Martin, *The Corinthian Body* (New Haven and London, Yale University Press, 1995).

Wayne A. Meeks, '"Since then you would need to go out of the world": Group Boundaries in Pauline Christianity', in T. J. Ryan, ed., *Critical History and Biblical Faith: New Testament Perspectives* (Billanova, Pa., College Theology Society, 1979), pp. 1–23.

Wayne A. Meeks, *The Origins of Christian Morality* (New Haven and London, Yale University Press, 1993).

Carlos Mesters, 'The Use of the Bible in Christian Communities of the Common People', in S. Torres and J. Eagleson, eds, *The Challenge of Basic Christian Communities* (New York, Orbis, 1981), pp. 197–210.

Daniel Migliore, *Faith Seeking Understanding* (Grand Rapids, Eerdmans, 1991).

Margaret M. Mitchell, *Paul and the Rhetoric of Reconciliation* (Louisville, Westminster/John Knox Press, 1993).

Walter Moberly, 'Did The Serpent Get It Right?', *Journal of Theological Studies*, NS, vol. 39 (1988), pp. 1–27.

Walter Moberly, '"Old Testament" and "New Testament": The Propriety of the Terms for Christian Theology', *Theology*, vol. XCV (1992), pp. 26–32.

Walter Moberly, *The Old Testament of the Old Testament* (Minneapolis, Fortress Press, 1992).

Jürgen Moltmann, *God in Creation* (London, SCM, 1985).

Robert Morgan, 'The Hermeneutical Significance of Four Gospels', in J. L. Mays, ed., *Interpreting the Gospels* (Philadelphia, Fortress Press, 1981), pp. 41–54.

Robert Morgan with John Barton, *Biblical Interpretation* (Oxford, Oxford University Press, 1988).

Robert Morgan, 'Faith', in *idem*, ed., *The Religion of the Incarnation* (Bristol, Bristol Classical Press, 1989), pp. 1–32.

# BIBLIOGRAPHY

Robert Morgan, 'Feminist Theological Interpretation of the New Testament', in Janet M. Soskice, ed., *After Eve. Women, Theology and the Christian Tradition* (London, Marshall Pickering, 1990), pp. 10–37.

Robert Morgan, 'On the Unity of Scripture', in Jon Davies *et al.*, eds, *Words Remembered, Texts Renewed* (Sheffield, Sheffield Academic Press, 1995), pp. 395–413.

Robert Morgan, 'Can the Critical Study of Scripture Provide a Doctrinal Norm?', *Journal of Religion*, vol. 76 (1996), pp. 206–32.

Jacob Neusner, *Torah Through the Ages* (London, SCM, 1990).

Thomas C. Oden, *After Modernity ... What?* (Grand Rapids, Zondervan, 1990).

Charles E. Reagan and David Stewart, eds, *Paul Ricoeur. An Anthology of his Work* (Boston, Beacon Press, 1978).

Christopher Rowland and Mark Corner, *Liberating Exegesis. The Challenge of Liberation Theology to Biblical Studies* (London, SPCK, 1990).

Jonathan Sacks, *The Persistence of Faith. Religion, Morality and Society in a Secular Age* (London, Weidenfeld and Nicolson, 1991).

Jonathan Sacks, *Faith in the Future* (London, Darton, Longman and Todd, 1995).

Sandra M. Schneiders, *The Revelatory Text. Interpreting the New Testament as Sacred Scripture* (San Francisco, HarperCollins, 1991).

Robin Scroggs, 'Paul and the Eschatological Woman', *Journal of the American Academy of Religion*, vol. 40 (1972), pp. 283–303.

Peter Selby, 'Who Is Really in Charge – Bible or Church?', in John V. Taylor *et al.*, *Bishops on the Bible* (London, Triangle/SPCK, 1993), pp. 32–52.

Nicola Slee, ed., *Testimony to Transformation. A Celebration of the Aston Training Scheme in its 18th year* (Birmingham, Aston Training Scheme, 1995).

James D. Smart, *The Strange Silence of the Bible in the Church* (London, SCM, 1970).

D. Moody Smith, *John* (Philadelphia, Fortress Press, 1976).

D. Moody Smith, *The Theology of the Gospel of John* (Cambridge, Cambridge University Press, 1995).

Janet Martin Soskice, 'Women's Problems', in Andrew Walker, ed., *Different Gospels. Christian Orthodoxy and Modern Theologies* (London, SPCK, 1993), pp. 194–203.

David M. Stanley, *Jesus in Gethsemane* (New York, Paulist Press, 1980).

David C. Steinmetz, 'The Superiority of Pre-Critical Exegesis', *Ex Auditu*, vol. 1 (1985), pp. 74–82, originally published in *Theology Today*, vol. 37 (1980), pp. 27–38.

Krister Stendahl, *The Bible and the Role of Women* (Philadelphia, Fortress Press, 1966).

John R. W. Stott, *Issues Facing Christians Today* (London, Marshall, Morgan and Scott, 1984).

# BIBLIOGRAPHY

R. S. Sugirtharajah, ed., *Voices from the Margin. Interpreting the Bible in the Third World* (London, SPCK, 1991).

John V. Taylor *et al.*, *Bishops on the Bible* (London, Triangle/SPCK, 1993).

John V. Taylor, 'Divine Revelation through Human Experience', in idem. *et al.*, *Bishops on the Bible* (London, Triangle/SPCK, 1993), pp. 1–11.

Gerd Theissen, *The Social Setting of Pauline Christianity* (Edinburgh, T & T Clark, 1982).

Anthony C. Thiselton, *The Two Horizons. New Testament Hermeneutics and Philosophical Description* (Grand Rapids, Eerdmans, 1980).

Marianne Meye Thompson, 'Intercession in the Johannine Community: 1 John 5.16 in the Context of the Gospel and Epistles of John', in M. J. Wilkins and T. Paige, eds, *Worship, Theology and Ministry in the Early Church* (Sheffield, JSOT Press, 1992), pp. 225–45.

Norman Todd, *A Thing Called Aston. An Experiment in Reflective Learning* (London, Church House Publishing, 1987).

Phyllis Trible, *God and the Rhetoric of Sexuality* (Philadelphia, Fortress Press, 1978).

Phyllis Trible, *Texts of Terror* (London, SCM, 1992).

Kevin J. Vanhoozer, 'The World Well Staged? Theology, Culture, and Hermeneutics', in D. A. Carson and J. D. Woodbridge, eds, *God and Culture. Essays in Honor of Carl F. Henry* (Grand Rapids, Eerdmans, 1993), pp. 1–30.

Rowan Williams, 'The Literal Sense of Scripture', *Modern Theology*, vol. 7 (1991), pp. 121–34.

John Wilson, 'Political Correctness', in Paul B. Clarke and Andrew Linzey, eds, *Dictionary of Ethics, Theology and Society* (London and New York, Routledge, 1996), pp. 651–4.

Miroslav Wolf, 'Soft Difference. Theological Reflections on the Relation Between Church and Culture in 1 Peter', *Ex Auditu*, vol. 10 (1994), pp. 15–30.

Charles M. Wood, *The Formation of Christian Understanding* (Philadelphia, Westminster, 1981).

N. T. Wright, *The New Testament and the People of God* (London, SPCK, 1992).

Frances Young, *The Art of Performance* (London, Darton, Longman and Todd, 1990).